SIMPLE
CHENILLE QUILTS

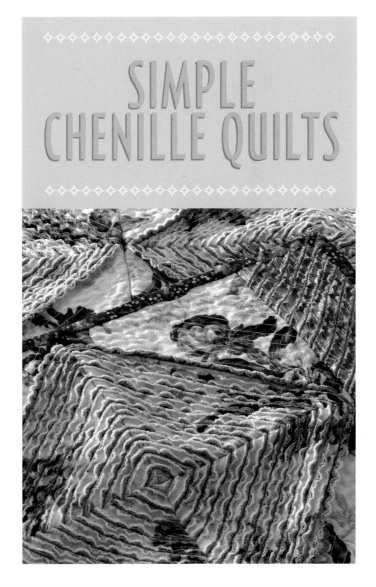

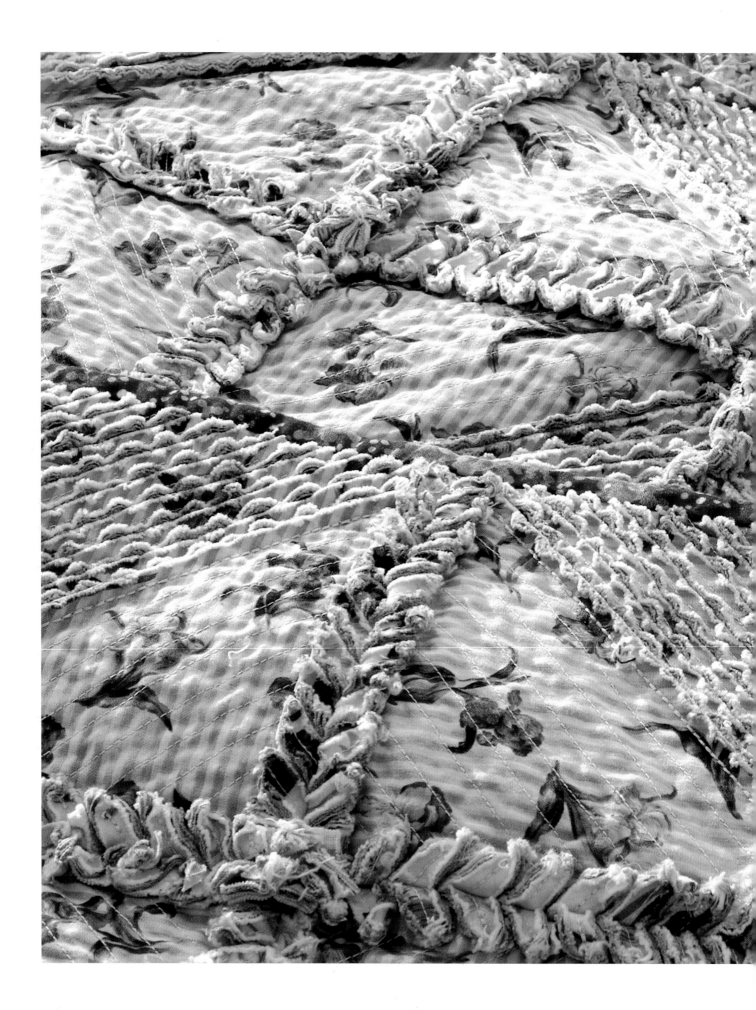

SIMPLE CHENILLE QUILTS
Block by Block

◇

AMY WHALEN HELMKAMP

Martingale®
& COMPANY

CREDITS

President · *Nancy J. Martin*
CEO · *Daniel J. Martin*
COO · *Tom Wierzbicki*
Publisher · *Jane Hamada*
Editorial Director · *Mary V. Green*
Managing Editor · *Tina Cook*
Technical Editor · *Darra Williamson*
Copy Editor · *Liz McGehee*
Design Director · *Stan Green*
Illustrator · *Robin Strobel*
Cover Designer · *Stan Green*
Text Designer · *Trina Craig*
Photographer · *Brent Kane*

Simple Chenille Quilts: Block by Block
© 2006 by Amy Whalen Helmkamp

That Patchwork Place® is an imprint of
Martingale & Company®.

Martingale & Company
20205 144th Avenue NE
Woodinville, WA 98072-8478 USA
www.martingale-pub.com

Printed in China
11 10 09 08 07 06   8 7 6 5 4 3 2 1

Library of Congress Cataloging-in-Publication Data
Library of Congress Control Number: 2006008464

ISBN-13: 978-1-56477-672-3
ISBN-10: 1-56477-672-7

MISSION STATEMENT

Dedicated to providing quality products and
service to inspire creativity.

DEDICATION

To my mother, whose love and faith in me is a constant in my life

ACKNOWLEDGMENTS

I would like to take this opportunity to thank those whose assistance helped make this book possible.

To Terry Martin and Karen Soltys, my sincere thanks for your encouragement and willingness to answer all my questions, no matter how small. I also want to include a thank-you to all the others at Martingale whose talents helped in the creation of this book.

Thank you to my friend Beth Ferrier, who has been my cheerleader throughout this process, giving me advice, uplifting my spirits when things seemed overwhelming, and recruiting some of the volunteers who lent their sewing skills to participate in the creation of the projects. My heartfelt thanks to those volunteers: Jeanne Aloia, Amanda Freeman, Isabel Lang, Valorie Scheer, and Audrey Vorich.

A big thank-you to my youngest daughter, Randi Adym, for making "For the Table." Your help and input were priceless to me.

Last but not least, my gratitude goes to the following fabric companies for their contributions to these projects: Northcott Silks, Inc. (fabric for quilts on pages 71, 77, 83, and 89), and RJR Fabrics (fabric for quilts on pages 36, 41, 49, 55, and 64).

Contents

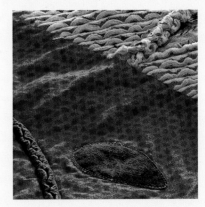

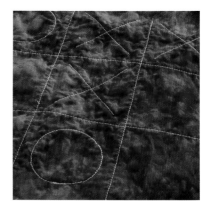

Preface

In January 2003, while riding along on the long drive to help my daughter move from Utah to Oregon, I let my mind wander, exploring different quilting techniques and possibilities. My thoughts rambled, jumping here and there, as ideas and designs began forming. The ideas came to me one on top of another; my mind raced with the possibilities. I knew some of these ideas would work and some would not. I made drawings and wrote mini-instructions in my sketchbook to try out later.

One idea in particular caught my attention. It combined two techniques—faux chenille and rag quilting. The pages of my sketchbook began to fill with design ideas and quickly written notes on how to construct the designs. As I worked out how to combine these two techniques to construct traditional block designs, the possibilities seemed endless. I was inspired, and *Simple Chenille Quilts* was begun.

I began experimenting with my ideas and loved the result. Now it's your turn to try your hand at creating these cuddlers. They are perfect to give or keep, and they will warm the hearts and bodies of all who receive them.

" . . . the possibilities seemed endless."

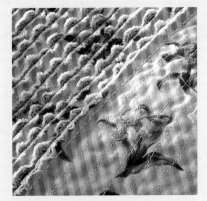

Introduction

A number of years ago, I learned a technique called faux chenille and found creating chenille fabric to be a fun and fascinating process. Usually what you start with looks nothing like the result. The resulting fabric is soft, cuddly, and oh-so-huggable!

A few years later, I learned a technique called rag quilting. The quilts made with this technique were quick and easy to piece. They were also soft and cuddly. It was a natural progression to combine these two techniques.

In this book, I will show you how to create chenille fabric and piece it using the rag-quilt method. The general directions at the beginning of the book include chenille-formula options, appliqué options, and finishing techniques. Quilting is done as you create the blocks, eliminating the need for quilting later.

Read all the instructions before you dive into the projects. Make some samples using the various chenille formulas. Unless otherwise noted, the patterns in this book can be created using any of these options. You'll want to know which formulas appeal to you and which don't before you invest your time and energy in creating each quilt.

Enjoy the process. Experiment with different fabrics and fillers, and I know you'll love the quilts you've created.

Glossary of Techniques

Faux Chenille: A method whereby you create chenille fabric by sewing multiple layers of fabric together with rows of stitching and then cutting between the rows of stitching through all but the base layer. The fabric sandwich is then washed and dried, which causes the cut fabric edges to fray and creates a chenille effect.

Rag Quilt: A quilt made up of blocks created by layering two fabrics wrong sides together (with an optional layer of flannel or batting in between), sewing one or two diagonal rows of stitching to secure the layers, and then sewing the blocks into rows, leaving the seams exposed. When the blocks have been joined and the rows sewn together, the exposed seams are clipped every ¼" to ½". The quilt is then washed and dried to fray the raw, clipped edges, causing the "rag" effect.

Chenille Rag Quilt: A quilt created by combining both of the techniques described above. The result is a quilt that is soft and cuddly, easy to construct, and reversible.

"I know you'll love the quilts you've created."

Fabrics

To make chenille, you'll need a base layer of fabric and additional layers of fabric for the chenille (filler and top layer). The number of layers used to make the chenille can vary, depending on the type of fabric(s) used. You'll learn more about this in "Chenille Formulas" on page 19.

Fabrics made from 100% cotton—including the majority of quilting cottons—are my number-one choice for all the layers made with this technique. Cotton fabrics come in a vast rainbow of colors, are durable, and—when cut on the bias—create a soft, plush chenille. Loosely woven and homespun cottons are good options. Fabrics that have been yarn dyed— that is, where the color is seen on both the right side and wrong side of the fabric—will produce a much bolder design. Fabrics that have been surface dyed will produce a softer-looking design.

For the inside layers of the chenille (the filler), you may use additional layers of the top-layer fabrics or introduce fabrics in a coordinating or contrasting color. Colored filler fabrics add depth to the chenille rows and bring out the patchwork design you create with the rows.

For a softer look, use muslin or osnaburg for the filler fabric. Muslin comes in bleached or unbleached finishes. Avoid using bleached muslin, which is preshrunk by the bleaching process. You'll also want to avoid any unbleached muslins that have been preshrunk by the manufacturer.

◇◇◇◇◇◇◇◇◇◇◇◇◇◇◇◇◇◇◇◇◇◇◇

Wait to Wash

Unless the project instructions tell you otherwise, *do not prewash any of the fabrics before use.* Prewashing removes the primary characteristic of the fabric—its tendency to shrink when washed—that helps to create good chenille. Also, if you must iron the fabrics, do so with a *dry* iron; steam will cause the fabrics to shrink.

◇◇◇◇◇◇◇◇◇◇◇◇◇◇◇◇◇◇◇◇◇◇◇

Osnaburg is best described as a coarse muslin. It creates a very plush chenille, making it a wonderful choice to use as a filler. It's a pale, oatmeal color and has a slightly rough texture and a lower thread count than muslin. Use one or two layers of osnaburg to add loft to your finished design. You may also combine a layer of muslin or osnaburg with colored filler layers.

Flannels are a wonderful choice for making chenille quilts. Use them for all the layers or as fillers. Flannel doesn't require lots of layers to create a nice chenille, and it frays up well with the rag technique. As with woven fabrics, avoid flannels that have been heavily dyed, or use these heavily dyed pieces as a base layer only.

"Cotton fabrics . . . create a soft, plush chenille."

Rayon is another fabric suitable for this technique. It's a soft, natural fiber, and it also comes in an array of colors. It "chenilles" well and gives a plush look to the design while reducing the weight of the project. Rayon, too, can be combined with other fabrics, such as cotton or flannel.

So what *isn't* a good candidate for this technique? Fabrics with a tight weave or those that are so heavily dyed that they feel stiff may not be the best choices; they may not produce the plush effect desired. I also don't recommend synthetic fabrics; they don't chenille well.

If you fall in love with a questionable fabric and feel that you just *must* use it, purchase a small amount and make a sample piece to see how the fabric performs. (In fact, I recommend that you make a test block with all the fabrics you plan to use. This is the best way to ensure success.) As an alternative, consider

"Flannels are a wonderful choice."

using the questionable fabric as a base layer rather than as one of the chenille layers.

Whichever fabrics you use, if you are worried about the possibility of the fabric bleeding, wash the finished quilt with a dye fixative, such as Retayne. You might also try a product called a dye magnet. Dye magnets absorb the excess dye from the wash water, preventing dye from settling on your quilt. If, too late, you discover that some dye has migrated from one fabric to another, you can wash the quilt again using a product such as Synthrapol to remove the excess dye. See "Resources" on page 95 for information about where to purchase these products.

Threads and Stitches

The threads used in making the chenille rag quilt serve a dual purpose: they hold the layers of fabrics together to create the chenille, and they add decorative interest in the non-chenille areas. You may choose threads in colors that coordinate or contrast with the fabric colors, depending on how much you want the stitching to show. Just be sure to choose threads that are of good quality. Although I prefer 100%-cotton threads, 100%-polyester threads are suitable also. Some of the new polyester threads have a beautiful sheen to them and will add a little sparkle to your project. Variegated threads also add visual interest.

Because you are stitching through multiple layers of fabric, I recommend using nothing smaller than a size 80/12 needle, with a size 90/14 being preferable. If you find that you are having tension problems, try a quilting needle or topstitch needle. Both have a larger eye and deeper groove than a regular needle to hold the thread while it passes through the multiple layers of fabric.

Always keep a good supply of sewing-machine needles handy. You'll do a lot of stitching as you make these projects, creating wear on the needle and affecting its performance. Changing the needle when necessary will ensure happier stitching.

There are just a few basic stitches used in these projects. You'll use a regular straight stitch for sewing the chenille rows. When you are making blocks with chenille on both sides, you'll use secure stitching on the guideline, which is addressed on page 18, to provide extra stability. Secure stitching can be a triple straight stitch (available on some machines) or two rows of straight stitching side by side.

To sew down appliqués, use either a straight stitch, zigzag stitch, or blind hem stitch. For an extra decorative touch in areas that have appliqués on one side of the block only, secure the appliqués with a triple straight stitch. If the fabric on the reverse side is a solid or tone-on-tone print, the stitching there will look like embroidery. See "Star of the Show" on page 55 and "Tic-Tac-Toe" on page 41 for examples.

Fusibles and Adhesives

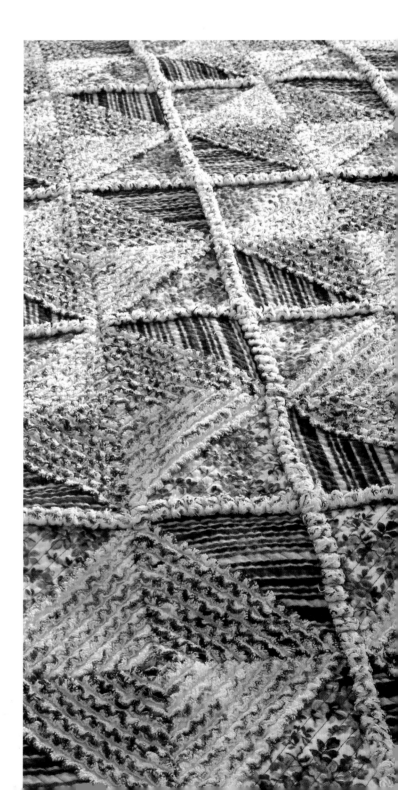

There are many fusible-web products on the market today, and most are suitable for the projects in this book. (The notable exception would be a no-sew fusible web, which tends to produce a stiffer end product.) Use your favorite fusible, or try one of my favorites such as Steam-A-Seam 2 Double Stick or Lite Steam-A-Seam 2 Double Stick (see "Resources" on page 95). I like the consistent results I have had when using these two products. Both may be purchased by the yard or as tape on a roll. Steam-A-Seam 2 Double Stick has the added feature of providing a permanent bond without needing to be stitched, though you can sew through it if desired. When using one of these fusible webs, always be sure to follow the manufacturer's directions. Failing to do so might result in poor performance of the product—and frustration for you.

Temporary adhesives are another alternative. These products come in a spray can, glue bottle, or glue stick and work well for holding down appliqués until they have been stitched. These adhesives also can be used to temporarily hold the layers of the fabric sandwich together as you stitch the rows for chenille. Again, follow the manufacturer's directions for the successful use of these products.

"Use your favorite fusible, or try one of my favorites."

Other Supplies

Before beginning any of these projects, make sure your sewing machine is in good working order. You'll be stitching through multiple layers of fabric, and a well-running machine is a necessity. Besides your sewing machine, you'll need the following basic supplies:

- **Rotary cutter, rotary ruler, and cutting mat for cutting out the pieces**

- **An erasable marker, marking pencil, or chalk for marking guidelines**

- **A small pair of sharp scissors with one rounded tip for cutting the chenille channels.** The blade with the rounded tip is the blade inserted into the channels. If you use scissors with two sharp tips, you may accidentally cut through the base layer, requiring you to remake the sandwich.

- **A walking foot for your sewing machine.** I *strongly* recommend that you use this attachment; it eliminates the shifting of the fabric layers as you stitch. Because you are sewing on multiple layers, the presser foot has a tendency to push the top layers of fabric forward as you sew. A walking foot provides a second set of feed dogs on these top layers, sandwiching them to the bottom layer so all layers move under the presser foot in unison.

- **Lots of straight pins.** Unless you are using a temporary adhesive (see page 13), you will need to pin baste the layers together in preparation for creating chenille, even when you use a walking foot. (If you are not using a walking foot, you'll need to use more pins to minimize the shifting of the layers as much as possible.)

I place the pins in the sandwiched block parallel to the stitched guideline, but you may prefer placing them perpendicular to the guideline. The most important thing is that the method you choose works well for you. Just remember to remove the pins as you come to them; don't sew over them.

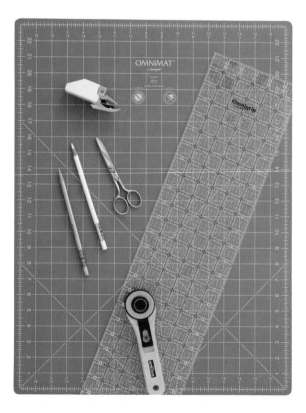

"... a well-running machine is a necessity."

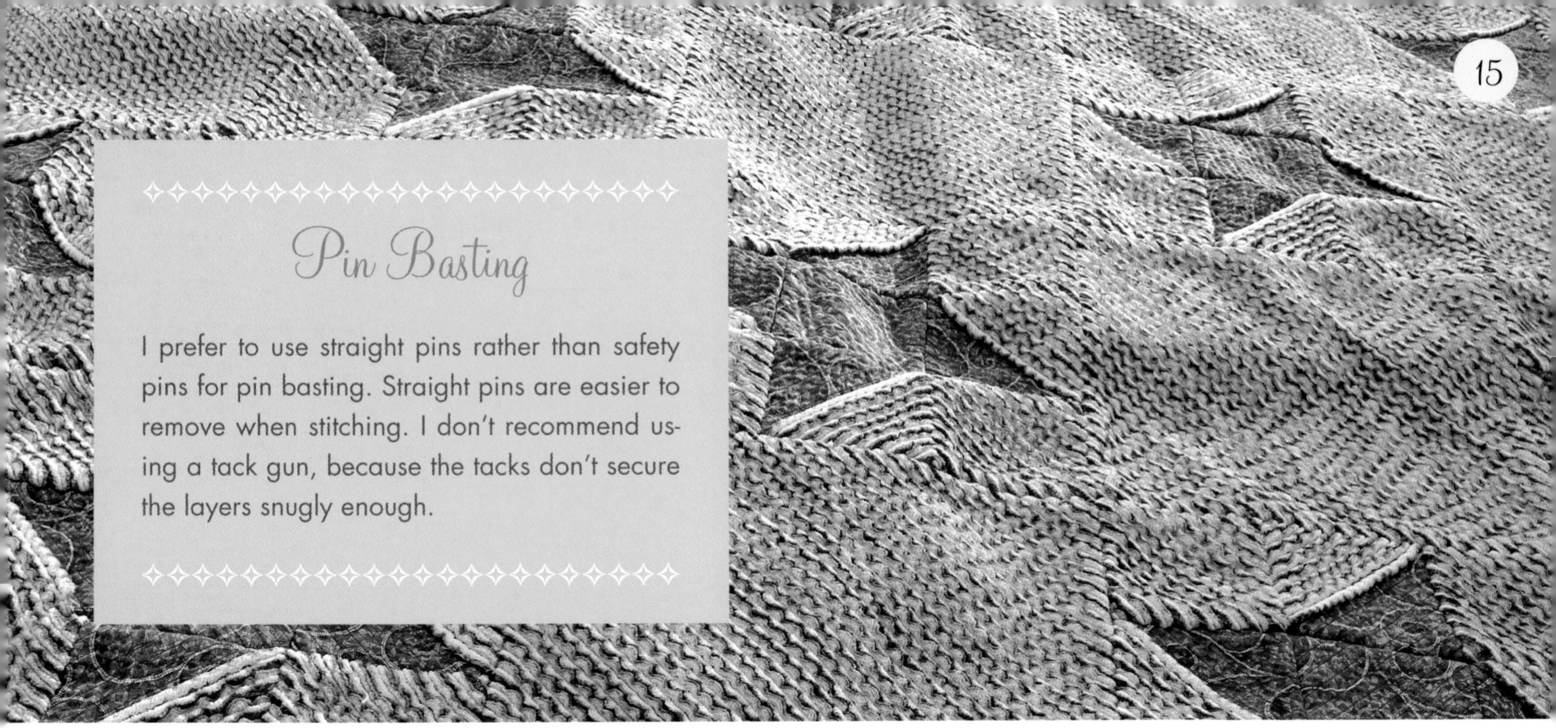

Pin Basting

I prefer to use straight pins rather than safety pins for pin basting. Straight pins are easier to remove when stitching. I don't recommend using a tack gun, because the tacks don't secure the layers snugly enough.

In addition to the necessities already listed, here are some optional tools you might like to consider.

- **A pair of rag scissors.** These are specialty scissors made just for cutting through many layers of fabric with ease.
- **A pair of electric scissors.** While not a necessity, they make cutting through the rows of chenille fast and easy. They are also a great help to those who have problems with arthritis or carpal tunnel syndrome.
- **A set of Omnistrips.** These narrow strips of rotary-mat material come in sets of three sizes to match the various sizes of channels you'll stitch when creating chenille. Simply insert an appropriately sized strip into the chenille channel and use a rotary cutter to cut down the center of the channel through all but the base layer. A word of warning: cut *carefully* so that you don't accidentally run the rotary cutter off the strip, cutting the block and nicking the edge of the strip. (Ask me how I know!)
- **A slash cutter.** On this specialized rotary cutter, the blade is located next to a guard that has a "finger" extending from it. The finger is inserted into the channel, and as the cutter is pushed through, the blade slashes through the fabric layers. This cutter comes in two styles: one with a short finger and one with a long finger. Here is how to use the cutter more effectively: make a ½" to 1" cut in the channel to make starting the slash easier, use steady, even pressure when pushing the cutter through the fabric, and occasionally clean the cutter to dislodge the threads and fuzz that get caught under the blade. (Do this *very carefully* because the blade is razor sharp!)

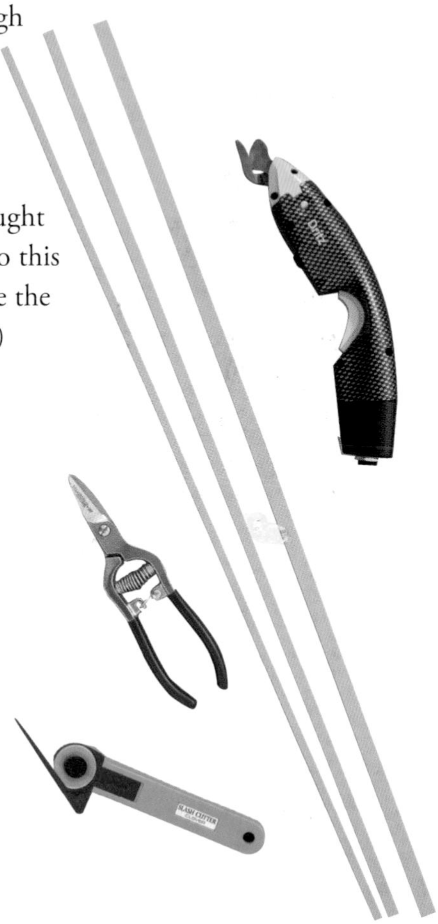

Chenille Techniques and Formulas

The process of creating chenille fabric is a simple one: stack layers of fabric together, sew evenly spaced rows of stitching, and then cut through all the fabric layers *except the base layer* between the stitched rows. Once you've mastered the basic technique, you can experiment with the various options.

CREATING CHENILLE FABRIC

Observe these simple guidelines to successfully create chenille.

- **Cut and sew on the bias.** Fabrics must be sewn and cut on a bias, typically at an angle that ranges between 30° and 60°. Failure to use the bias results in chenille that is stringy rather than plush; the threads of the fabrics become unwoven rather than frayed. For the projects in this book, you'll stitch at a 45° angle—the true bias of woven fabrics.

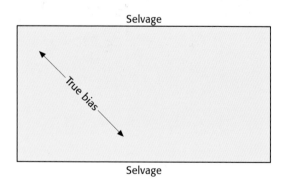

- **Maintain the correct spacing between lines of stitching.** For cotton fabrics, the distance between the rows of stitching must measure between ¼" and ½". The number of layers used for the chenille as well as the type of fabrics you use will determine how far apart to make the rows. This is why making a test block is so important! It allows you to see what the product will look like and gives you a chance to make adjustments as needed.

  In general, rayon and woven cottons must be stitched every ¼" to ⅜". Flannels and osnaburg can be stitched every ⅜" to ½".

- **Launder your chenille.** You must wash and dry the finished chenille; you won't see the fruits of your labor until you've done so. It's the process of getting the fabric wet and then drying it in a hot dryer that allows the cut edges to reveal their hidden beauty. This step creates lots of lint in the dryer, so check and clean the lint trap of your dryer frequently.

- **Enlarge the base layer for one-sided chenille; match the base-layer size for two-sided chenille.** As I mentioned earlier, to make chenille, you'll need a base layer of fabric and additional layers of fabric for the chenille. The number of layers will vary depending on the type of fabric(s) used. For blocks with chenille on one side only, cut the base layer 1" larger than the chenille layers, and center the chenille layers on the base layer for stitching. The difference in size makes it easier to insert the scissors into the channel for cutting the chenille. In blocks with chenille on both sides, cut the base layer the same size as the chenille layers.

- **Use assembly-line methods.** Assembly-line sewing will speed up the stitching process and save *lots* of thread. With this method, you'll stitch two blocks at a time. Sew the first line of stitching on the guideline (see page 18) of the first block. Without removing the block, place the next block under the presser foot, and stitch the guideline on the new block.

Chain-piece blocks in pairs for speedier stitching.

When you reach the end of the second block, cut the first block loose, bring it to the front and, using the first line of stitching as your guide, continue with the next row of stitching. Repeat this process until you've completed all the rows of stitching on both blocks.

Align rows of stitching across both blocks.

As your stitching progresses across each block, you'll overlap the two blocks more and more to line up the next line of stitching.

Continue assembly-line sewing two blocks at a time until you've stitched the required number of blocks for the project you are making. To cut the chenille, use a sharp pair of scissors or your preferred cutting tool to cut down the center of the channels between the rows of stitching, being careful not to cut the base layer.

- **Reshape distorted blocks.** Once you've cut all the channels, you may find that the block has become a bit distorted. You can fix this by holding the block at the corners and pulling gently in the same direction as the stitching. Work your way along the sides, too, until the block has been pulled back into shape.

To correct the shape of a distorted block, gently pull in the direction of the stitching.

"The process of creating chenille fabric is a simple one."

MAKING A SAMPLE BLOCK

Follow the steps below to make a sample block. The fabrics, cut sizes, and stitching distances are just suggestions for the purpose of practice. You'll ultimately determine the block measurements and spacing based on the project you choose and on the fabrics and number of layers that you use.

1. Cut one 8" x 8" square of cotton fabric for the base layer.
2. Cut three 7" x 7" squares of cotton fabric for the chenille layers (filler and top layer).
3. Place the base layer right side down and center the remaining layers right side up on top of the base layer. Pin baste the layers together.

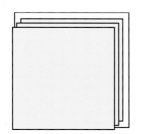

4. Use an erasable marker to draw a diagonal stitching guideline on the top square from the upper-left to the lower-right corner.

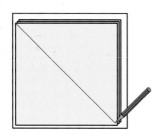

5. Sew the first line by stitching directly on the guideline you drew in step 4. Using this line of stitching as a guide, sew the remaining lines of stitching, spacing them ⅜" apart.

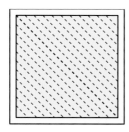

Space the rows ⅜" apart.

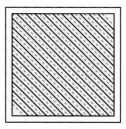

Spacing Rows Evenly

I use the presser foot on my sewing machine as a guide for spacing the rows, and this works even if the rows are not ¼" apart. Another option is to use your ruler and marker to draw all the stitching lines onto the block.

6. Use a small, sharp pair of scissors with one rounded tip to cut the channels between the rows of stitching through all the chenille layers of fabric. *Do not cut into the base layer.* Trim the excess fabric from the perimeter of the base layer.

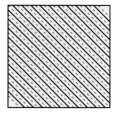

Cut between the rows of stitching.

Trim the excess base layer.

"You'll be amazed at what you see!"

Caution!

Be sure that the rounded scissor blade is *between* the base layer and the top layers, or this might happen to you!

Keeping Fabrics Flat

If the cut chenille layers get caught on the presser foot, use a stiletto to keep the fabrics flat. Another option is to place a strip of tissue paper or tear-away stabilizer over the seam area before sewing it. Remove the tissue paper/stabilizer when you're finished sewing.

7. Repeat steps 1–6 to make three more sample squares. Referring to steps 6 and 7 of "Making a Rag-Quilt Sample" on page 22, arrange and sew the squares as shown to make a Four Patch block. Sew a line of stitching ¼" from the raw edge all the way around the block.

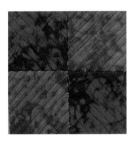

8. Once you've finished your sample chenille block, it's time to wash and dry it. This is the exciting part: it causes the fabric to shrink and the cut edges to "bloom" (or fray). When you remove the block from the dryer, you'll be amazed at what you see! Your flat block now has texture in the form of plush rows of chenille. Notice how soft the fabrics have become. These features make chenille perfect for creating cuddler quilts for the people you care about.

CHENILLE FORMULAS

Other than observing the fabric-content requirements for making chenille, what you do from here is pretty much up to you. Experimenting with different colors, different numbers of layers, and different combinations of fabrics and colors in the layers are the variables that make creating chenille so much fun. Ask yourself "I wonder what would happen if . . . ?" to see what you can come up with. The number of fabrics that you layer will vary, based on the type of fabric(s) you are using. Start out with these basic combinations, make a sample of each for reference, and go from there.

Woven Cottons or Rayon

Start with four layers—one for the base layer and three for the chenille. Make one block using the same fabric for all four layers, and then make one using different colors for the layers of chenille filler. On each block, space the rows of stitching ¼" apart on half of the block and ⅜" apart on the other half.

Flannel

Start with three layers—one for the base layer and two for the chenille. Make a second block using four layers—one for the base layer and three for the chenille. Again, experiment with mixing colors in the layers of chenille filler. On each block, space the rows of stitching ⅜" apart on half of the block and ½" apart on the other half.

Muslin

Start with four layers—one for the base layer and three for the chenille. Make a second block with five layers—one for the base layer and four for the chenille. On each block, space the rows of stitching ¼" apart on half of the block and ⅜" apart on the other half to see the different results. Imagine how pretty an entire quilt made with muslin chenille blocks would be. Try using contrasting thread for stitching the chenille rows to add another decorative effect.

Osnaburg

Because of its slightly rough feel, I recommend using osnaburg only as a filler layer. Make several blocks, mixing osnaburg with woven cottons, flannels, or muslin. Start with a minimum of three fabric layers, making the osnaburg the filler and using other fabrics for the base and top layers. Space the rows of stitching ¼" apart on half of the block and ⅜" apart on the other half. Make a second block, using two layers of osnaburg for the filler (four layers total) and spacing the stitching ⅜" and ½" apart. Notice the difference in the density of the chenille.

Batting

Yes, batting can be used as a filler to create chenille, although I don't recommend using it for more than one layer. Use *only* good-quality cotton batting in a medium weight. There will be lots of exposed areas of the batting, and a product of lesser quality won't hold up. Make a test block using two layers of fabric—one for the base layer and one for the top layer, placing the batting in between. Space the rows of stitching ¼" to ⅜" apart.

For more information on creating chenille, I recommend Nannette Holmberg's book *New Directions in Chenille* (Martingale and Company, 2000).

Making Test Blocks

The projects in this book call for blocks with anywhere from three to five layers of fabric. It's important to make test blocks with the different numbers of layers to see if you'll have any problems when it comes time to sew the blocks together. Blocks with 3 layers will have seam intersections that consist of 12 layers; blocks with 5 layers will have seam intersections consisting of 20 layers. See "Quilt Assembly" on page 27 for tips on coping with these multiple layers. If you still experience problems sewing over all the layers, try reducing the number of layers called for in the project. One layer can be eliminated from the quilts that call for 5 layers. For quilts made with flannel and that have 4 or 5 layers, you can reduce the number of layers to as few as 3 (1 for the base layer and 2 for the chenille). The reverse is also an option; if you wish, you can *add* a layer or two to the stack. Experiment with your machine and your fabrics to learn to make the best choices.

Rag Technique

ag edge, frayed edge, raw edge, and *rag quilting:* all of these terms refer to simple techniques that leave the seam and cut edges of the fabrics exposed on the outside of the quilt. The best fabrics for this technique are flannels and homespun cottons.

To make a rag quilt, squares are traditionally cut 1" larger than the finished block (that is, 7" x 7" for a 6" x 6" finished block). The block pieces are placed wrong sides together, with an optional layer of fabric, flannel, or batting sandwiched between and stitched from corner to corner on both diagonals, creating an X through the block. The blocks are then sewn together with a ½" seam allowance left exposed on one side of the quilt. Once the rows are joined, the seams are clipped every ½". To finish the outside edge of the quilt, a line of stitching is sewn ½" from the edge, and the outside edge is clipped as well.

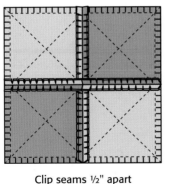

Clip seams ½" apart almost to stitching line.

The next step is to wash and dry the quilt. This will cause those clipped seams to fray, thus the name "rag quilt." Remember, this process also creates lots of lint, so check your dryer lint trap two or three times during drying.

MAKING A RAG-QUILT SAMPLE

Follow these simple steps to make the blocks for a sample rag quilt. The fabrics, cut sizes, and stitching

Clipping Seam Allowances

Seam allowances can be clipped in one of two ways. You can clip the seams as you sew blocks together, or you can wait and clip all the seams after the quilt is assembled. I prefer to clip as I go, but the choice is yours.

distances are suggestions for the purpose of practice and will yield a 6" x 6" finished block. Ultimately, blocks may be whatever size you wish. Just remember to add 1" to the desired finished size for the seam allowances when you cut the fabric squares.

1. Cut two 7" x 7" squares. These can be cut from the same fabric or two different fabrics.

2. Place the two squares from step 1 wrong sides together. If desired, cut a 7" x 7" flannel square and sandwich it between the two squares. Pin baste the layers together.

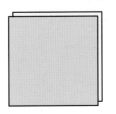

Two layers

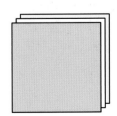

Two layers with optional flannel layer

3. Use an erasable marker to draw a diagonal line from the upper-left corner to the lower-right corner and from the lower-left corner to the upper-right corner on the top layer. These are your stitching guidelines.

4. Sew the layers together by stitching on the guidelines you drew in step 3.

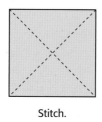

Stitch.

5. Repeat steps 1–4 to make three more sample squares.

6. Sew the blocks into two rows of two blocks each so that all the seams show on one side of the row.

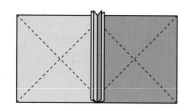

7. Sew the rows together, once again keeping all the seams on one side of the unit.

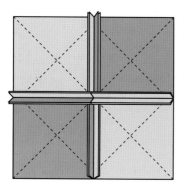

8. Sew a line of stitching ½" from the raw edge all around the outside edge of the quilt.

9. Clip all the seams, including those around the outside edge. Space the clips ½" apart, and stay at least ⅛" from the stitching line.

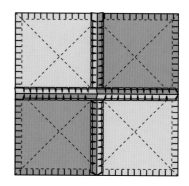

10. Finally, wash and dry the sample quilt. This causes the clipped seams to fray, giving the quilt the shaggy "rag look." Now, notice how soft the quilt has become—perfect (in a larger size, of course!) for covering up with while reading a good book, watching TV, or taking that afternoon siesta.

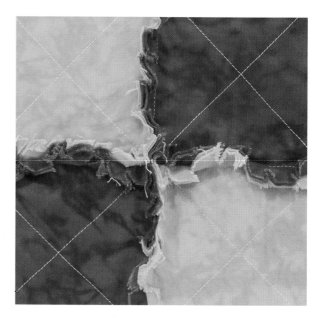

For more information and ideas for creating rag quilts, I recommend Evelyn Sloppy's book *Frayed-Edge Fun: 10 Cozy Quilts* (Martingale and Company, 2002).

Appliqués

Adding appliqués to a quilt is like decorating a room. Appliqués can add that little extra touch that makes your project complete. Whether flat or three-dimensional, simple or complex, subtle or bold, appliqués can be an accessory or the main focus of the design. The choice is up to you.

The method you choose to attach those appliqués is also up to you. They can be sewn on by hand or machine, or "glued" on using a fusible web. Whichever method you prefer is fine.

CREATING APPLIQUÉS

There are a number of different ways to make appliqués. I mention a few of my favorites here.

Make a paper template of the appliqué. Trace the design onto a piece of paper and cut out the paper shape. Pin the paper template onto the wrong side of the fabric and trace around it. For hand or invisible machine appliqué, such as a blind hem stitch, cut out the appliqué adding ¼" all around. For raw-edge or zigzag-stitch machine appliqué, cut out the appliqué directly on the traced line.

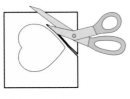

Cut ¼" outside drawn line.

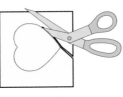

Cut on drawn line.

Make a template of the appliqué from freezer paper. Trace the appliqué onto the paper side of the freezer paper and cut out the paper shape. Using a dry iron on a medium-high heat setting, iron the freezer-paper shape shiny side down on the wrong side of the fabric. For hand or invisible machine appliqué (i.e., blind hem stitch), cut out the appliqué, adding ¼" all around. For raw-edge or zigzag-stitch machine appliqué, cut out the appliqué right along the edge of the paper template, and then remove the freezer paper.

◇◆◇◆◇◆◇◆◇◆◇◆◇◆◇◆◇◆◇◆◇◆◇◆◇

Pressing Freezer Paper

When pressing a freezer-paper template, press just long enough so that the freezer paper adheres to the fabric—about 5 to 10 seconds. It should peel off easily. If it doesn't, either press for a shorter length of time or lower the heat setting on your iron.

◇◆◇◆◇◆◇◆◇◆◇◆◇◆◇◆◇◆◇◆◇◆◇◆◇

Use a fusible web. Trace the shape onto the fusible web and cut out the shape directly on the traced line. For large appliqué shapes, cut out the center area of the motif, leaving ¼" of web inside the traced

"Appliqués can add that little extra touch that makes your project complete."

design. This eliminates the stiffness that can result when an appliqué is fused. Apply the webbed side of the fusible to the wrong side of the fabric, following the manufacturer's directions. Cut out the shape right along the outside edge of the fusible.

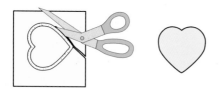

Use fusible tape. Fusible tape is simply a narrow strip of fusible web. It can be used to apply stems, vines, or three-dimensional appliqués. Follow the manufacturer's directions for its use.

MAKING YO-YOS

A yo-yo is a three-dimensional circle that is fun and easy to make. To cut the shape, decide the finished size (diameter) you would like your yo-yo to be, double that measurement, and add ¼". For example, to make a 2" yo-yo, cut a circle template 4¼" (2" x 2" + ¼") in diameter.

1. Make a circle template the desired size, trace it onto either side of the fabric, and cut out the fabric shape directly on the traced line.

2. Turn under ¼" to the wrong side of the fabric circle and use a needle and doubled thread to do a running stitch all around the outside edge, overlapping the first stitch by two or three stitches.

3. Pull the thread tight. This will gather the outside edge of the circle, pulling it in toward the center with the turned-under edge on the inside. Tie off and clip the thread. Flatten the yo-yo so the gathered edge is in the center of the circle. Your

yo-yo is now complete and ready to be attached, gathered side up, to your quilt or other project.

There are several different ways to attach a yo-yo to your quilt.

- It may be tacked down by sewing a few stitches on the outside edge. Use a large running stitch that catches the underside of the yo-yo, securing it to the project.
- Place a few stitches in the center of the yo-yo, catching the edge of the small opening left when the circle was gathered.
- Use a washable fabric glue to secure it down.
- Finally, but less desirably because it will flatten the yo-yo, use a small piece of fusible web or tape and iron the yo-yo to the project surface.

MAKING CHENILLE STRIPS

Chenille strips make great appliqués. They add texture as well as decoration to your project. Use them alone or to surround another appliqué or a motif printed on the fabric. The method for making chenille strips is very similar to the method you use to make a chenille block. Experiment with different fabrics and combinations to see which ones you prefer.

1. With right sides up, place three or more identically sized pieces of fabric one on top of another. Pin baste the layers together.

2. Draw a 45° diagonal line from the top edge to the bottom edge. This is the stitching guideline. Depending upon whether your sandwich is a square or rectangle, this line may span from corner to corner—or it may not.

45° guideline

3. Sew directly on the drawn line. Using this stitched line as a guide, continue sewing parallel rows of stitching across the block, spacing the rows consistently from ¼" to ½" apart. The distance between rows will depend on how wide you want the strips to be, what type of fabrics you are using, and how many layers you are sewing through. Do some experimenting to see which "formulas" you like best.

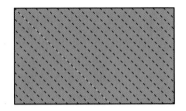

4. When you are finished sewing all the rows, cut the block into strips by cutting down the center of the channels between the stitched rows *through all layers.* Square off both ends of each strip by cutting off the tips.

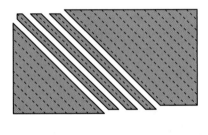

To use the chenille strips, simply stitch them in place by sewing down the center of the strip on top of the existing stitching. Either backstitch or sew five to six tiny stitches at the beginning and end of each strip to secure the strip in place. If you find that a partially sewn strip is not long enough, stop stitching as you approach the end, slip another strip under it so the ends overlap by about ¼", and continue sewing.

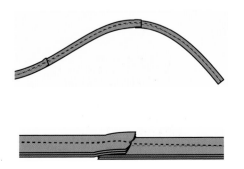

ADDING THE APPLIQUÉS

There are many ways to attach an appliqué to your project, and many books on the market describing these ways. *The Easy Art of Appliqué* by Mimi Dietrich and Roxi Eppler (That Patchwork Place, 1994) is a good reference. Use your favorite method or try one of the following with appliqués made as described in "Creating Appliqués" on page 23.

For a finished edge, use an appliqué cut according to the paper method or freezer-paper method and include a ¼" seam allowance. Fold the seam allowance over the edge to the back of the paper template and press.

Sew the appliqué to the block by hand with a ladder stitch or by machine, using a narrow zigzag or blind hem stitch. Choose a thread that matches the appliqué or, for added interest, one that contrasts with the appliqué fabric. Be sure to remove the paper template before sewing down the last inch or two of the appliqué.

To make the ladder stitch, thread a needle with a single strand of thread. Knot the thread and bring the needle up from the back of the block to the front. Insert the needle into the folded edge of the appliqué, and then push the needle back into the block right next to where it emerged. Travel ⅛" on the reverse side of the block and bring the needle back up through the block, inserting it through the folded edge of the appliqué. Repeat until you've stitched around the entire appliqué. Tie off the thread on the reverse side of the block.

To secure the appliqué by machine using a narrow zigzag stitch, set your stitch width to a setting of 1 to 2 (approximately ⅛" to ¹⁄₁₆") and your stitch length to a setting of 1 to 2 (15 to 18 stitches per inch). If you prefer the blind hem stitch, set the stitch width to a setting of 1 to 2 (approximately ⅛" to ¹⁄₁₆"). With either stitch, you want the needle to take just a tiny bite into the appliqué and then fall just off the edge of the appliqué into the background fabric. If these stitches are kept narrow, they will give the appearance of hand stitching.

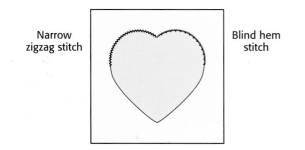

If you use a fusible web, follow the manufacturer's directions carefully. Failing to do so could result in a poor bond. Note that not all fusible webs can be sewn, so be sure to check the directions carefully. To protect your iron, always use a press cloth when applying appliqués with a fusible web. Depending on which fusible web you've chosen, you may need to stitch the appliqué down after fusing. Use either a narrow zigzag stitch or straight stitch sewn close to the edge of the appliqué to secure the edges.

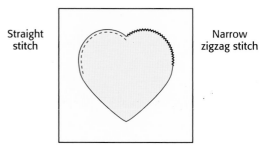

The rules that apply to fusible webs also apply to fusible tapes. Read the manufacturer's directions carefully. Tapes can be used in small pieces to tack down an appliqué or three-dimensional appliqué until it is sewn down, or in longer strips to fuse down stems and vines. Tapes can also be used to apply chenille strips to the project. Again, some fusible tapes will need to be sewn down, and some won't.

Quilt Assembly

Once all the blocks have been made, it's time to put the quilt together. The process is much the same as assembling a traditionally pieced quilt top that would later be layered with batting and backing and then quilted. However, there are three big differences with the projects in this book:

- These quilts are quilted as you make them.
- All blocks and rows are sewn together using a ½" seam allowance.
- When the blocks and rows are pieced, the seams are left exposed on one or both sides of the quilt. You then clip the seams every ½" or use the chenille cuts as your guide.

  Follow the directions carefully so the seams end up on the correct side of the quilt. Because you are working with multiple layers of fabric, the seams may be an issue when it comes time to sew the rows together. Here are some tips to help you sew more smoothly through these multiple layers:

- *Slow down!* Don't try to barrel through all those layers. Keep your machine running at a steady pace. Once you've gotten over the seam, you may pick up speed again until you reach the next seam.
- Try using a height-compensation tool (some call it a seam jumper or a hump jumper). This is a device that you place under the foot attachment to raise the foot up to the thickness you are about to sew. It helps prevent the foot from getting hung up on the bulky seams.

- I learned this next trick at my local quilt shop during one of the shop's sewing-club meetings. It really does work! Get a clean hammer (yes, I said a hammer) and a small, clean block of wood. Open the end of the seam, place it on the block of wood, and hit the seam a few times with the hammer. This does two things: it flattens the seam and softens the fabric.

◇◇◇◇◇◇◇◇◇◇◇◇◇◇◇◇◇◇◇◇◇◇◇◇

Caution!

Do not try the hammer-and-wood method on your sewing table/cabinet. You don't want to accidentally hit your machine!

◇◇◇◇◇◇◇◇◇◇◇◇◇◇◇◇◇◇◇◇◇◇◇◇

- Make a clip in the seam allowance. Clip the seam ½" from the raw edge—the distance from the edge that you sew. With the seam clipped, the needle has fewer layers to sew through. Don't clip any closer than ⅛" from the stitching line.

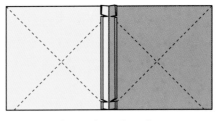

Clip ½" from the edge.

Finishing

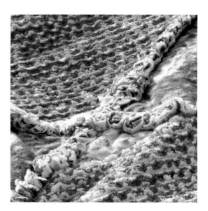

Because the pieces are already quilted, you are left with one final step to finish your quilt. You have two choices: a rag edge or a standard straight-of-grain or bias binding. The first provides a look that coordinates with the rag-edge seams; the latter gives a more finished look. Both are suitable for the projects in this book. Although instructions for each project are written using one method or the other, you may choose either method. Just remember that you'll need binding fabric if you choose to substitute binding on a rag-edge project.

RAG EDGE

You can follow through with the "rag quilt" look by treating the outside edge of your quilt the same as you treat the seams.

1. Sew a line of stitching ½" from the edge all around the outside edge of the assembled quilt. When you come to a seam, finger-press it open before sewing over it.

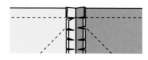

2. Clip every ½" along the raw edge to within ⅛" of the stitching line. If the blocks along the outside edge are chenille, you may use the chenille cuts as your guide for making these clips.

3. Wash and dry the quilt as directed on page 30. It's as simple as that!

BINDING

If you would like to give your quilt a more finished look, you can add a standard binding. You may cut the binding by using one of the following two methods.

Straight-of-Grain Binding

1. From the binding fabric, cut the required number of 2½"-wide strips from the crosswise straight of grain. Trim off the selvages.

2. Place the ends of two strips right sides together at a right angle. Stitch diagonally from the upper-left to the lower-right corner of the top strip as shown. Trim the excess, leaving a ¼" seam allowance, and press the seam open. Repeat to make one continuous long strip.

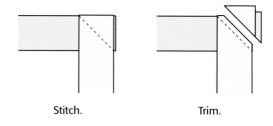

Stitch.   Trim.

3. Fold the completed binding strip in half lengthwise, wrong sides together, and press.

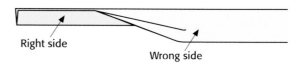

Right side   Wrong side

4. Place the binding right sides together on the quilt, making sure the raw edges are aligned. Leaving the first 12" of binding free, sew the binding to the quilt with a ¼" seam allowance. Stitch to within ¼" of the corner. Stop with the needle in the down position.

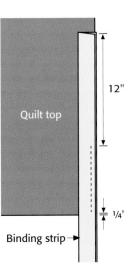

5. Raise the presser foot, turn the quilt a quarter turn (90°), and backstitch off the edge of the quilt.

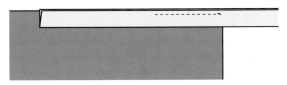

6. Raise the presser foot and remove the quilt from the machine. Flip the binding up so that it's parallel with the next side to be stitched as shown.

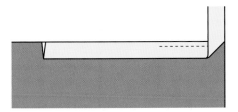

7. Flip the binding down so that the folded edge is even with the edge of the quilt. Resume stitching at the edge of the quilt as shown. Repeat at each corner; your binding will have perfectly mitered corners when the entire process is complete.

8. After turning the last corner, stitch to within approximately 24" of where you started. Remove the quilt from beneath the presser foot. Overlap the ends of the binding, measure, and trim off the excess so that the end overlaps the beginning of the binding by 2¼".

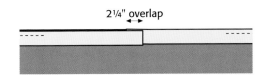

9. Open the two ends of the binding strip. With right sides together, join the ends using the method described in step 2. Trim away the excess fabric, leaving a ¼" seam allowance.

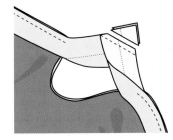

10. Finger-press the seam allowance open, refold the binding strip, and finish sewing it to the edge of the quilt.

11. Wrap the binding around to the back of the quilt, encasing the seam allowance, and pin the binding in place. At each corner, fold the binding on the back to form a mitered corner. Hand or machine stitch the binding to secure.

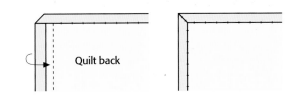

Bias Binding

1. Unfold the binding fabric so that it's flat and either right or wrong side up. Bring the upper-left corner down to the center fold line to create a diagonal fold across the upper-left side of the fabric.

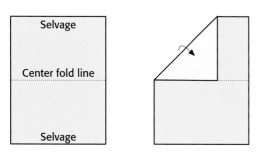

2. Bring the lower-right corner up to the fold line to create a diagonal fold across the lower-right side of the fabric.

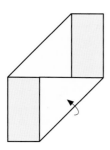

3. Bring the two folded edges together as shown. The sides will not be even.

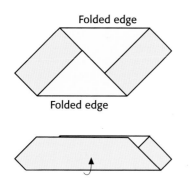

4. Place your ruler so that it is perpendicular to the folded edge and use a rotary cutter to cut the required number of 2½"-wide strips from the fabric.

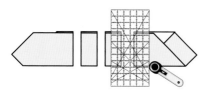

5. Square off the ends of the strips. Piece them together and sew the binding to the quilt, following steps 2–11 of "Straight-of-Grain Binding" on pages 28–29.

WASHING AND DRYING THE QUILT

At last, your quilt is ready for the final step! This is where all the "magic" happens. The process of washing and drying the quilt makes the chenille "bloom" and the clipped seams fray. As mentioned earlier, you'll need to check the quilt throughout this process as there will be a great deal of lint created not only in the dryer, but also in the wash water. This is especially true if the quilt is made of flannel.

Place the quilt in the washer with the water level set at its highest level. Add just a small amount of detergent to help remove any sizing from the fabrics. Use a dye magnet or a product such as Retayne to help set the dyes (see "Resources" on page 95). Set the timer for the shortest wash cycle and start the machine. After the washer has completed the wash cycle, drained the water, and gone through the first spin cycle, *turn off the machine* and check for excess lint on the wall of the tub. Remove this buildup and *close the lid* before restarting the machine. Let the machine complete the washing cycle, and then remove the quilt and shake it out. No doubt, you'll find bits of lint clinging to the quilt. Remove them before putting the quilt into the dryer. Because of all the layers, the quilt will take a fair amount of time to dry. During this process, remember to check the lint trap in your dryer several times to remove the lint buildup.

Once the quilt is dry, give it a good shake to fluff it up. Next, it will need a "haircut"—some strings in the seams will need to be trimmed. Simply clip the strings off with a pair of scissors.

Now your chenille rag quilt is ready to enjoy. I hope you have as much fun with this technique as I have had. The possibilities are endless if you maintain a "What if?" attitude and let your imagination be your guide.

DIAMONDS

Made by
Amy Whalen Helmkamp

These diamonds are created not by Mother Nature but by sewing and assembling chenille squares made with three printed flannels and an ecru flannel for the filler. When all of the squares are joined, diamonds appear on both the front and back of the quilt, which makes it not only soft and cuddly but also reversible.

Finished Quilt: 49" x 73" (before washing)
Finished Block: 12" x 12"

FRONT SIDE

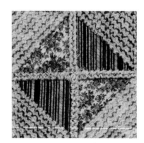

REVERSE SIDE

MATERIALS

All yardages are based on 42"-wide fabric. **Do not prewash fabrics.**

- 11½ yards of ecru flannel for filler
- 4 yards of small-scale floral print flannel for blocks
- 3 yards of narrow-striped flannel for blocks and binding
- 2⅛ yards of mottled-print flannel for blocks
- 4 spools of thread, each 500 meters (547 yards), in a coordinating color
- Refer to "Other Supplies" on page 14.

CUTTING

Cut all strips across the width of the fabric (selvage to selvage) unless instructed otherwise.

From the narrow-striped flannel, cut:
10 strips, 7" x 42"; crosscut into 48 squares, 7" x 7"
2½"-wide bias strips to equal 256"*

From the ecru flannel, cut:
58 strips, 7" x 42"; crosscut into 288 squares, 7" x 7"

From the flannel with small-scale floral print, cut:
20 strips, 7" x 42"; crosscut into 96 squares, 7" x 7"

From the mottled-print flannel, cut:
10 strips, 7" x 42"; crosscut into 48 squares, 7" x 7"

You must cut these strips on the bias for the stripes to run diagonally. Refer to "Bias Binding" on page 30 for guidance as needed.

MAKING THE BLOCKS

You'll make 24 blocks for this quilt. Each block is made up of four squares. Each square consists of five layers of flannel. As you cut the chenille, *pay very close attention* to the number of layers you are cutting. You don't want to cut through the base layer.

Use a ½" seam allowance throughout the block construction. Use the chenille cuts as a guide when clipping the seam allowances. Refer to "Chenille

Techniques and Formulas" on page 16 for guidance as needed.

1. Layer a 7" striped square right side down, three 7" ecru squares right side up, and a 7" floral square right side up. Pin baste the layers. Make 48 and label them *square A.*

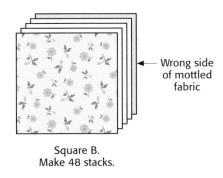

Square A.
Make 48 stacks.

2. Repeat step 1, substituting the 7" mottled squares for the striped squares. Make 48 and label them *square B.*

Square B.
Make 48 stacks.

3. Use an erasable marker to draw a diagonal line from the upper-left corner to the lower-right corner on the floral side of each A square sandwich as shown. This will be your stitching guideline. Repeat for each B square.

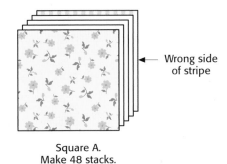

4. Select one marked A square. Use a walking foot to sew a line of stitching directly on the guideline you marked in step 3. Continue sewing rows of stitching parallel to the guideline as shown. On one half of the square, space the rows of stitching ⅜" apart. On the other half of the square, space the rows of stitching ½" apart. Repeat for all A and B squares.

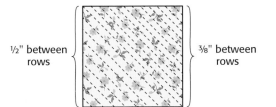

½" between rows   ⅜" between rows

5. On the floral side of each A square, cut the center of the ⅜"-wide channels through *the top two layers only.* On the striped side, cut the center of the ½"-wide channels through *the top two layers only.* Make 48.

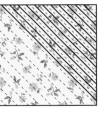 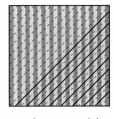

Cut the center of the ⅜"-wide channels.   Cut the center of the ½"-wide channels.

Square A.
Make 48.

6. On the mottled side of each B square, cut the center of the ⅜"-wide channels through *the top two layers only.* On the floral side, cut the center of the ½"-wide channels through *the top two layers only.* Make 48.

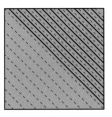 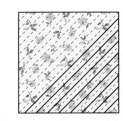

Cut the center of the ⅜"-wide channels.   Cut the center of the ½"-wide channels.

Square B.
Make 48.

7. Place the floral side of one A square and the mottled side of one B square right sides together so the cut halves face each other. Sew the squares together. Clip the seam allowances. Finger-press the seams open at each end. Make 48.

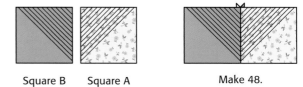

Square B   Square A   Make 48.

8. Place the floral/mottled sides of two units from step 7 right sides together, with the cut areas facing each other. Sew the units together. (Refer to "Quilt Assembly" on page 27 for tips on sewing through multiple layers.) Clip the seam allowances. Finger-press the seams open at each end. Make 24 blocks.

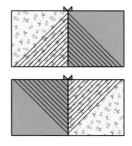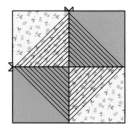

Front side of block.
Make 24.

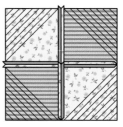

Reverse side of block

ASSEMBLING THE QUILT

Use a ½" seam allowance throughout the quilt construction. Refer to "Quilt Assembly" on page 27 for tips on sewing through the multiple layers created when seaming pieces together. Use the chenille cuts as a guide when clipping the seam allowances.

1. Referring to the quilt diagram at right, arrange the blocks in six horizontal rows of four blocks each as shown. Place the blocks so that the long seam (i.e., the last seam sewn) in the block runs vertically and will be parallel to the seam that joins the blocks. With floral/striped sides together, sew the blocks into rows. Clip the seam allowances as you go. Finger-press the seams open at each end. Make six rows.

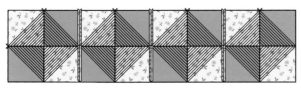

Make 6 rows.

2. With floral/striped sides together, sew the rows into pairs. Clip the seam allowances and finger-press the seams open at each end. Make three pairs. Repeat to sew the pairs of rows together, clip the seam allowances, and finger-press.

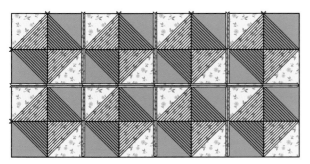

Make 3.

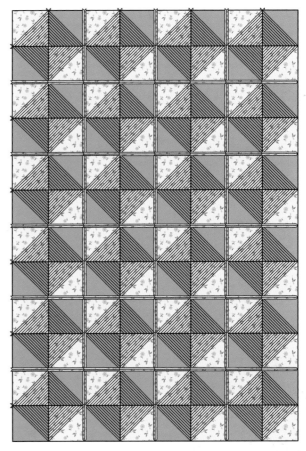

Quilt diagram

FINISHING THE QUILT

Refer to "Finishing" on page 28 for instructions on making and applying the narrow-striped bias binding, and washing and drying the quilt.

FUZZY RAILS

Made by
Jeanne Aloia

Most rail fences are made to surround a field, holding the animals that graze within, but these rails are made to surround the recipient with comfort and warmth. Anyone would enjoy being "fenced in" by this quilt while watching TV, reading a good book, or taking that afternoon nap.

Finished Quilt: 55" x 73" (before washing)
Finished Block: 9" x 9"

FRONT SIDE OF BLOCK

REVERSE SIDE OF BLOCK

MATERIALS

All yardages are based on 42"-wide fabric. **Do not prewash fabrics.**

- 7⅝ yards *each* of dark red, dark blue, and hunter green tone-on-tone print for blocks and filler
- 2 spools of thread, each 500 meters (547 yards), in each fabric color (6 spools total)
- Refer to "Other Supplies" on page 14.

CUTTING

Cut all strips across the width of the fabric (selvage to selvage).

From the dark red tone-on-tone print, cut:
6 strips, 11" x 42"; crosscut into 16 rectangles, 11" x 13"
16 strips, 12" x 42"; crosscut into 48 rectangles, 10"x 12"

From the dark blue tone-on-tone print, cut:
6 strips, 11" x 42"; crosscut into 16 rectangles, 11" x 13"
16 strips, 12" x 42"; crosscut into 48 rectangles, 10" x 12"

From the hunter green tone-on-tone print, cut:
6 strips, 11" x 42"; crosscut into 16 rectangles, 11" x 13"
16 strips, 12" x 42"; crosscut into 48 rectangles, 10" x 12"

MAKING THE BLOCKS

You'll make 48 blocks for this quilt. Each block is made up of three rectangles: one red, one blue, and one green. Each rectangle consists of four layers of fabric. As you cut the chenille, *pay very close attention* to the number of layers you are cutting. You don't want to cut through the base layer.

Use a ½" seam allowance throughout the block construction. Use the chenille cuts as a guide when clipping the seam allowances. Refer to "Chenille Techniques and Formulas" on page 16 for guidance as needed.

1. Layer one 11" x 13" red rectangle right side down and three 10" x 12" red rectangles right side up, centering them so that ½" of the base layer extends all around. Pin baste the layers. Mark the top red rectangle to identify it as the one on which you'll create the chenille, and label it *side 1*. Make 16.

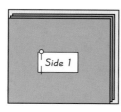

Make 16.

2. Repeat step 1, substituting the blue rectangles for the red rectangles. Make 16.

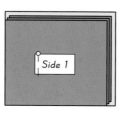

Make 16.

3. Repeat step 1, substituting the green rectangles for the red rectangles. Make 16.

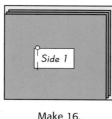

Make 16.

4. Use an erasable marker to mark the bottom edge of the top (red, blue, or green) rectangle 10" from the lower-left corner on side 1 of each unit from

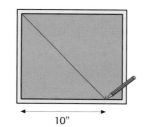

steps 1–3. Draw a diagonal line from the upper-left corner to this mark as shown. This will be your stitching guideline.

5. Select one marked rectangle. Use a walking foot to sew a line of stitching directly on the guideline you marked in step 4. Continue sewing rows of stitching parallel to the guideline. Space the rows of stitching ⅜" apart. Repeat for all red, blue, and green rectangles.

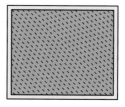

Stitch rows ⅜" apart.

6. On side 1 of each unit from step 5, cut the center of the ⅜"-wide channels through *the top three layers only*. Trim the excess base layer.

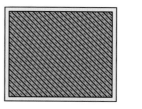 

Cut the center of the ⅜"-wide channels.

7. Working along the 12" side, cut each rectangle from step 6 into three smaller rectangles, 4" x 10", as shown. Make 144 rectangles, 48 of each color.

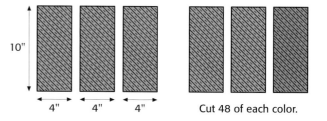

Cut 48 of each color.

8. Layer a red rectangle and a green rectangle cut side up. Sew the rectangles together along the right edge. Clip the seam allowances. Finger-press the seams open at each end. Make 48.

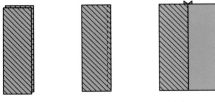

Make 48.

9. Layer a blue rectangle, cut side down, on the uncut side of the green rectangle in each unit from step 8. Sew the rectangles together along the right edge. Clip the seam allowance and finger-press. Make 48.

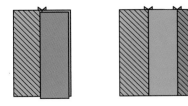

Make 48.

ASSEMBLING THE QUILT

Use a ½" seam allowance throughout the quilt construction. Refer to "Quilt Assembly" on page 27 for tips on sewing through the multiple layers created when seaming pieces together. Use the chenille cuts as a guide when clipping the seam allowances. Refer to the quilt diagram on page 40 for guidance as needed.

1. Place one block, red and blue cut sides up, with the rails running horizontally and with the red rail on top as shown. Place a second block beside the first, with the red and blue cut side up, the rails running vertically, and with the red rail on the right.

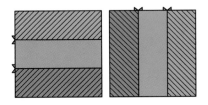

2. Without changing the orientation of the blocks, place the first block, with red and blue cut side up, on top of the second block. Sew the blocks together along the right edge. Clip the seam allowances. Finger-press the seams open at each end. Make 12.

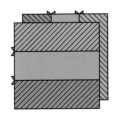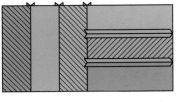

Make 12.

3. Sew three pairs from step 2 together to make a row as shown. Make four rows and label them rows *1, 3, 5,* and *7.*

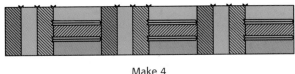

Make 4
(rows 1, 3, 5, and 7).

4. Place one block, green cut side up, with the rails running vertically and with the red rail on the left as shown. Place a second block, green cut side up, with the rails running horizontally and with the red rail on top.

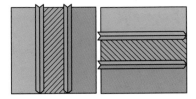

5. Without changing the orientation of the blocks, place the first block, green cut side up, on top of the second block. Sew the blocks together along the right edge. Clip the seam allowances. Finger-press the seams open at each end. Make 12.

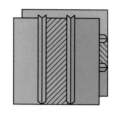

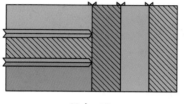

Make 12.

6. Sew three pairs together to make a row as shown. Make four rows and label them rows *2, 4, 6,* and *8.*

Make 4
(rows 2, 4, 6, and 8).

7. Sew a row from step 3 and a row from step 6 together to make a pair. Clip the seam allowances and finger-press the seams open at each end. Make four pairs. Sew the pairs of rows together, clip the seam allowances, and finger-press.

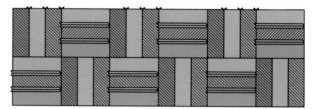

Make 4.

Quilt diagram

FINISHING THE QUILT

Refer to "Finishing" on page 28 for instructions on creating a rag-edge finish, and washing and drying the quilt.

"These rails are made to surround the recipient with comfort and warmth."

TIC-TAC-TOE

Made by Amy Whalen Helmkamp

Remember the childhood games we played on the school blackboard during recess—hangman, connect the dots, and tic-tac-toe? This quilt is reminiscent of those games of tic-tac-toe. Seldom did anyone win, but we played the game over and over. This charming quilt is sure to evoke pleasant memories for the one who receives it.

Finished Quilt: 58" x 70" (before washing)
Finished Block: 15" x 15"

FRONT SIDE

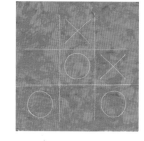

REVERSE SIDE

MATERIALS

All yardages are based on 42"-wide fabric. **Do not prewash fabrics unless otherwise noted.**

- 5 yards of dark red mottled print for sashing and borders
- 4⅓ yards of osnaburg for chenille strips and filler*
- 2⅞ yards of blue mottled print for sashing and borders
- 2½ yards of black mottled print for blocks
- ⅞ yard of cream mottled print for chenille strips
- 1 fat quarter *each* of 9 different brightly colored mottled prints for blocks
- 1 spool of cream thread, 500 meters (547 yards), for chenille strips
- 1 spool of black thread, 150 meters (164 yards), for sashing
- Refer to "Other Supplies" on page 14.

Wash this fabric after cutting 2 strips, 12" x 42, from the crosswise grain (see "Cutting" below). Secure the cut edges of the fabric with a zigzag stitch before washing.

CUTTING

Cut all strips across the width of the fabric (selvage to selvage) unless instructed otherwise. Follow the cutting directions precisely to ensure that you have enough yardage to cut all the necessary pieces.

From the unwashed osnaburg, cut:
2 strips, 12" x 42"

From the *lengthwise grain* of the prewashed osnaburg, cut:
1 strip, 7" x 116"; crosscut into 2 strips, 7" x 58"*
9 squares, 16" x 16"

From the cream mottled print, cut:
2 strips, 12" x 42"

From *each* of the brightly colored mottled prints, cut:
1 square, 16" x 16" (9 total)

From the black mottled print, cut:
5 strips, 16" x 42"; crosscut into 9 squares, 16" x 16"

From the *lengthwise grain* of the blue mottled print, cut:
2 strips, 7" x 58"

From the remaining blue mottled print, cut:
5 squares, 17" x 17"
4 rectangles, 9" x 17"

From the *lengthwise grain* of the dark red mottled print, cut:
2 strips, 7" x 58"

From the remaining dark red mottled print, cut:
15 squares, 16" x 16"
12 rectangles, 8" x 16"

Unfold the fabric to make a single layer before cutting these strips.

MAKING THE CHENILLE STRIPS

Refer to "Making Chenille Strips" on page 24 for guidance as needed.

1. Layer the two 12" x 42" osnaburg strips and the two 12" x 42" cream strips right side up as shown. Pin baste the layers.

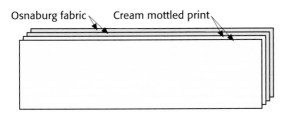

2. Use the 45° marking on your ruler and an erasable marker to draw a 45° line in the approximate center of the fabric stack from step 1 as shown. This will be your stitching guideline.

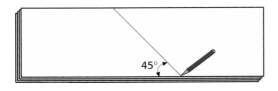

3. Using a walking foot, sew a line of stitching directly on the guideline you marked in step 2. Sew four or five more lines of stitching parallel to the guideline. Space the rows of stitching ½" apart. Stop and cut the center of one channel, cutting through *all layers of the fabric*. This creates two separate, more manageable pieces to work with.

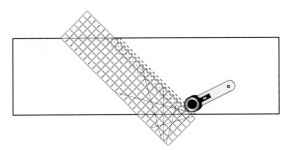

Cut the center of one ½"-wide channel.

4. Continue sewing parallel rows of stitching ½" apart until you've filled both pieces. Cut the center of the ½"-wide channels through *all layers of the fabric* to create chenille strips as shown. Trim the tips of each strip.

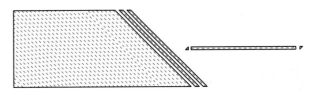

MAKING THE BLOCKS

You'll make nine blocks for this quilt. Each block consists of three layers of fabric. You'll appliqué the newly made chenille strips to the blocks to create the tic-tac-toe boards and pieces.

1. Layer a 16" bright print square right side down, a 16" osnaburg square, and a 16" black square right side up. Instead of pin basting these squares, I used a temporary spray adhesive to hold them together. This made it easier to twist and turn the block during the appliqué process; there were no pins to catch. Make nine.

Make 9.

2. Use an erasable marker to mark the top edge of the top (black) square 6" from the upper-left corner of each unit from step 1. Using this point as a guide, measure down 2" and draw a 12"-long vertical line. Draw a second 12"-long line 4" to the right of and parallel to the first line as shown.

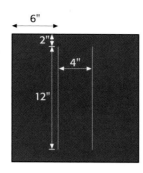

3. Mark the left edge of the top (black) square 6" from the lower-left corner of each unit. Using this point as a guide, measure in 2" and draw a 12"-long horizontal line. Draw a second 12"-long line 4" above and parallel to the first line as shown.

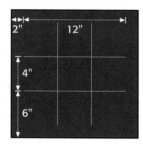

4. Refer to the photo on page 41. Follow the layout shown or devise one of your own and use the patterns on page 48 to mark *X*s and *O*s on each block.

5. Appliqué chenille strips to cover the horizontal and then the vertical grid lines on each block. Finish by appliquéing chenille strips over the marked *X*s and *O*s.

Using a Decorative Stitch

To create the decorative look of embroidery on the reverse side of the blocks, use a securing stitch, such as the triple straight stitch, to sew down the strips. See "Threads and Stitches" on page 12 for guidance as needed.

MAKING THE SASHING AND CORNER SQUARES

You'll make a total of 24 sashing strips and 16 corner squares for this quilt. Each unit consists of four layers of fabric. As you cut the chenille, *pay very close attention* to the number of layers you are cutting. You don't want to cut through the base layer.

1. Layer a 17" blue square right side down and three 16" red squares right side up, centering them so that ½" of the base layer extends all around. Pin baste the layers together. Make five.

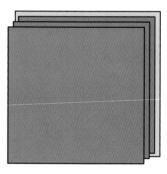

Make 5.

2. Now use an erasable marker to draw a diagonal line from the upper-left corner to the lower-right corner on the red side of each unit from step 1. This will be your stitching guideline.

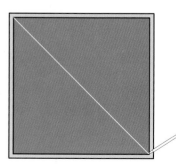

3. Select one marked unit from step 2. Use a walking foot to sew a line of stitching directly on the guideline you marked in step 2. Continue sewing rows of stitching parallel to the guideline. Space the rows ⅜" apart. Repeat for all units from step 2.

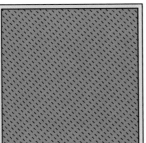

Stitch rows ⅜" apart.

4. On the red side of each unit from step 3, cut the center of the ⅜"-wide channels through *the top three layers only.* Trim the excess base layer. Make five.

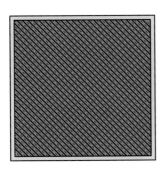

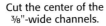

Cut the center of the
⅜"-wide channels.

Make 5.

5. Layer a 9" x 17" blue rectangle right side down and three 8" x 16" red rectangles right side up. Pin baste the layers together. Make four.

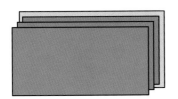

Make 4.

6. Use an erasable marker to mark the bottom edge of the top (red) rectangle 8" from the lower-left corner of each unit. Draw a diagonal line from the upper-left corner to this mark as shown. This will be your stitching guideline.

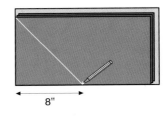

8"

7. Select one marked unit from step 6. Use a walking foot to sew a line of stitching directly on the guideline you marked in step 6. Continue sewing rows of stitching parallel to the guideline. Space the rows ⅜" apart. Repeat for all units from step 6.

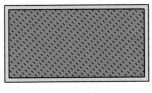

Stitch rows ⅜" apart.

8. On the red side of each unit from step 7, cut the center of the ⅜"-wide channels through *the top three layers only.* Trim the excess base layer. Make four.

Cut the center of the
⅜"-wide channels.

Make 4.

9. Lay out the square and rectangle units so that the chenille cuts all run in the same direction: from the upper-right corner to the lower-left corner. This will ensure consistency when the sashing is sewn in place.

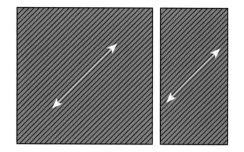

10. Use a rotary cutter and ruler to cut one 16" square from step 4 into sixteen 4" squares as shown. Cut each remaining 16" square into four 4" x 16" strips (16 total).

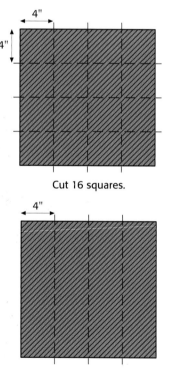

Cut 16 squares.

Cut 16 strips.

11. Cut each rectangle from step 8 into two 4" x 16" strips (8 total).

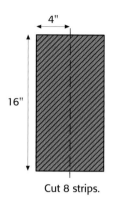

Cut 8 strips.

MAKING THE BORDERS

You'll make two borders for this quilt. Each border consists of three layers of fabric. You'll appliqué the remaining chenille strips to the borders to create the tic-tac-toe pieces.

1. Layer a 7" x 58" red strip right side down, a 7" x 58" osnaburg strip, and a 7" x 58" blue strip right side up. I used a temporary spray adhesive to hold the layers together during the appliqué process. Make two.

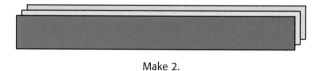

Make 2.

2. Measure and use an erasable marker to draw a vertical line at the center of each unit from step 1. Mark three additional lines, 8¼" apart, to the left and right of this centerline. These are your placement guides for the appliquéd Xs and Os.

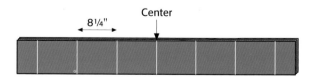

3. Referring to the quilt diagram at lower right and using the patterns on page 48, draw the Xs and Os onto the marked border sandwiches, alternating them as shown. Appliqué the chenille strips over the marked Xs and Os.

ASSEMBLING THE QUILT

Use a ½" seam allowance throughout the quilt construction. Refer to "Quilt Assembly" on page 27 for tips on sewing through the multiple layers created when seaming pieces together. Use the chenille cuts as a guide when clipping the seam allowances.

1. Referring to the assembly diagram below, arrange the appliquéd squares black side up, the sashing strips red side up, and the corner squares red side up as shown.

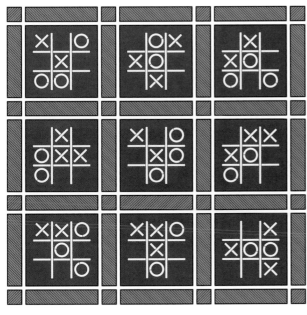

Assembly diagram

2. With red sides together, sew four corner squares and three sashing strips together. Clip the seam allowances and finger-press the seams open at each end. Make four sashing rows.

Make 4.

3. With red and black sides together, sew four sashing strips and three blocks together. Clip the seam allowances and finger-press the seams open at each end. Make three block rows.

Make 3.

4. With red and black sides together, sew the rows together. Clip the seam allowances and finger-press the seams open at each end.

5. With appliquéd sides of the border and appliquéd sides of the quilt top together, sew a border to the top and bottom of the quilt. Clip the seam allowances and finger-press the seams open at each end.

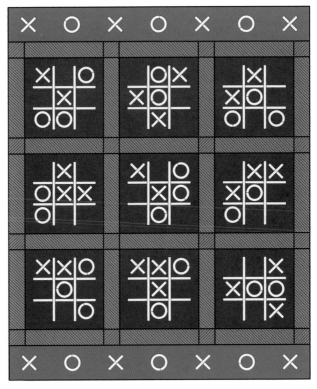

Quilt diagram

FINISHING THE QUILT

Refer to "Finishing" on page 28 for instructions on creating a rag-edge finish, and washing and drying the quilt.

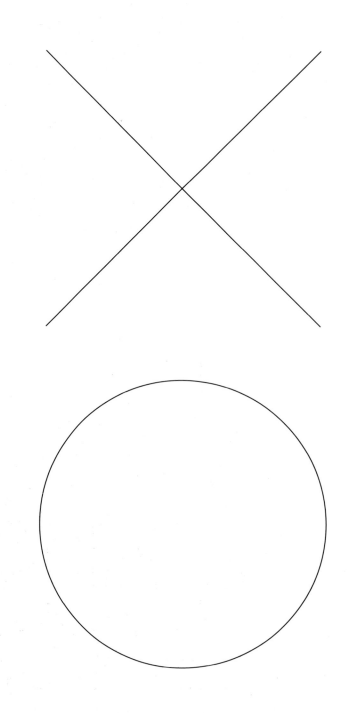

FOREVER FRIENDS

Made by Amy Whalen Helmkamp

✧✧✧✧✧✧✧✧✧✧✧✧✧✧✧✧✧✧✧✧✧✧

I love to gaze up at the night sky and marvel at the celestial bodies that have resided there since ... forever. Just like those stars, some friendships are meant to last forever. Let that special friend know how much you care by creating this blanket of stars as a gift. It will remind her of you each time she crawls beneath it to "sleep under the stars."

✧✧✧✧✧✧✧✧✧✧✧✧✧✧✧✧✧✧✧✧✧✧

Finished Quilt: 61" x 85" (before washing)
Finished Block: 12" x 12"

FRONT SIDE

REVERSE SIDE

MATERIALS

All yardages are based on 42"-wide fabric. **Do not prewash fabrics.**

- 7¼ yards of dark blue print for blocks and binding
- 5½ yards of medium blue print for blocks
- 5½ yards *each* of light yellow print and dark yellow print for filler
- 5½ yards of osnaburg fabric for filler (optional)
- 5 spools of thread, each 500 meters (547 yards), in a coordinating color
- Refer to "Other Supplies" on page 14.

CUTTING

Cut all strips across the width of the fabric (selvage to selvage).

From the dark blue print, cut:
9 strips, 14" x 42"; crosscut into 17 squares, 14" x 14"
11 strips, 10" x 42"; crosscut into 41 squares, 10" x 10"
8 strips, 2½" x 42"

From the light yellow print, cut:
6 strips, 13" x 42"; crosscut into 17 squares, 13" x 13"
11 strips, 10" x 42"; crosscut into 41 squares, 10" x 10"

From the (optional) osnaburg fabric, cut:
6 strips, 13" x 42"; crosscut into 17 squares, 13" x 13"
11 strips, 10" x 42"; crosscut into 41 squares, 10" x 10"

From the dark yellow print, cut:
6 strips, 13" x 42"; crosscut into 17 squares, 13" x 13"
11 strips, 10" x 42"; crosscut into 41 squares, 10" x 10"

From the medium blue print, cut:

6 strips, 13" x 42"; crosscut into 17 squares,
    13" x 13"

11 strips, 10" x 42"; crosscut into 41 squares,
    10" x 10"

MAKING THE BLOCKS

You'll make 35 blocks for this quilt: 17 solid chenille blocks and 18 Nine Patch Star blocks. Each block is made up of five layers of fabric. (The osnaburg layer is optional; eliminate it if you wish.) As you cut the chenille, *pay very close attention* to the number of layers you are cutting. You don't want to cut through the base layer.

Use a ½" seam allowance throughout the block construction. Use the chenille cuts as a guide when clipping the seam allowances. Refer to "Chenille Techniques and Formulas" on page 16 for guidance as needed.

Solid Chenille Blocks

1. Layer a 14" dark blue square right side down, a 13" light yellow square right side down, a 13" osnaburg square (optional), a 13" dark yellow square right side up, and a 13" medium blue square right side up, centering them so that ½" of the base layer extends all around. Pin baste the layers. Make 17.

Make 17.

2. Use an erasable marker to draw a diagonal line from the upper-left corner to the lower-right corner on the medium blue side of each unit from step 1. This will be your stitching guideline.

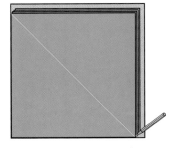

3. Select one marked square. Use a walking foot to sew a line of stitching directly on the guideline you marked in step 2. Continue sewing rows of stitching parallel to the guideline. Space the rows of stitching ⅜" apart. Repeat for all squares.

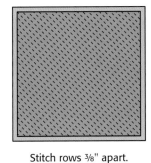

Stitch rows ⅜" apart.

4. On the medium blue side of each square, cut the center of the ⅜"-wide channels through *the top four layers only (three layers if you omitted the osnaburg layer).* Trim the excess base layer.

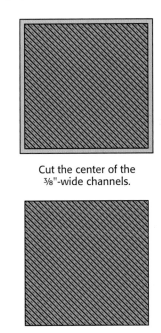

Cut the center of the
⅜"-wide channels.

Nine Patch Star Blocks

Each block is made up of nine 5" squares. Note that the dark blue (base) layer is the same size as the other layers. This is because some of the squares have chenille on both sides.

1. Layer the 10" dark blue, light yellow, osnaburg (optional), dark yellow, and medium blue squares

as described in "Solid Chenille Blocks," step 1, on page 51. (The edges of the squares will match.) Make 41.

Make 41.

2. Use an erasable marker to draw a diagonal line from the upper-left corner to the lower-right corner on the medium blue side of each unit from step 1. This will be your stitching guideline.

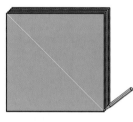

Make 41.

3. Divide the units from step 2 into two stacks: one with 36 units and one with 5 units.

4. Begin with the stack of 36 units. Referring to "Threads and Stitches" on page 12, use a walking foot to sew a line of secure stitching directly on the guideline you marked in step 2. Continue sewing rows of *regular* straight stitching (not secure stitching) parallel to the guideline. Space the rows of stitching ⅜" apart. Repeat for all 36 units.

Secure stitching

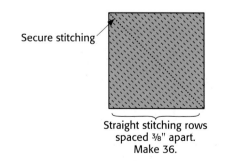

Straight stitching rows spaced ⅜" apart.
Make 36.

5. Using a rotary cutter and ruler, cut each unit from step 4 into four 5" squares (144 total). Separate the squares with secure stitching into one stack and

the rest into another stack. Label the squares with secure stitching *square A* and the squares without secure stitching *square B*. You'll have 72 of each.

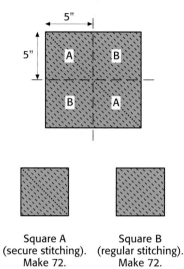

Square A
(secure stitching).
Make 72.

Square B
(regular stitching).
Make 72.

6. On the dark blue side of each A square, cut the center of the ⅜"-wide channels on one half of the square through *the top four layers only (three layers if you omitted the osnaburg layer)*. Make 72.

Square A.
Cut the center of the
⅜"-wide channels.
Make 72.

7. On the medium blue side of each A square, cut the center of the ⅜"-wide channels on the other half of the square through *the top four layers only (three layers if you omitted the osnaburg layer)*. Make 72. When the quilt is washed, each side of this unit will look as though it were pieced with half-square triangles.

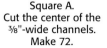

Square A.
Cut the center of the
⅜"-wide channels.
Make 72.

8. On the medium blue side of each B square, cut the center of the ⅜"-wide channels through *the* *top four layers only (three layers if you omitted the osnaburg layer).* Make 72.

Square B.
Cut the center of the
⅜"-wide channels.
Make 72.

9. Select one marked unit from the remaining five units from step 3. Use a walking foot to sew a line of stitching directly on the guideline you marked in step 2. Continue sewing rows of stitching parallel to the guideline. Space the rows ⅜" apart. Repeat for all five units.

Stitching rows
spaced ⅜" apart

10. On the medium blue side of each unit from step 9, cut the center of the ⅜"-wide channels through *the top four layers only (three layers if you omitted the osnaburg layer).*

Cut the center of the
⅜"-wide channels.

✧✧✧✧✧✧✧✧✧✧✧✧✧✧✧✧✧✧✧✧✧

Quicker Stitching

If you wish, you can use assembly-line piecing to construct the blocks (see page 16).

✧✧✧✧✧✧✧✧✧✧✧✧✧✧✧✧✧✧✧✧✧

11. Using a rotary cutter and ruler, cut each unit from step 10 into four 5" squares (20 total). You'll use 18 squares for the Nine Patch Stars; label them *square C.* Save the 2 extras for another project.

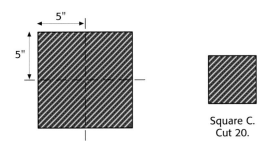

Square C.
Cut 20.

12. Separate the 5" squares into nine stacks, laying them out as shown. Pay close attention to the direction of the cuts on each cut square and the direction of the rows of stitching on the uncut squares as well.

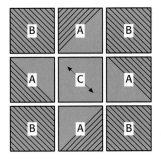

Arrow indicates direction of stitching.

13. Beginning with row 1, place the first two squares with medium blue sides together and sew them together. Clip the seam allowances. Finger-press the seams open at each end. Make 18. Repeat to sew the first two squares of row 2 (medium blue sides together) and the first two squares of row 3 together as shown.

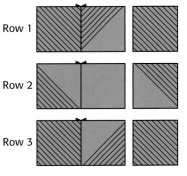

Row 1
Row 2
Row 3

Make 18 of each row.

14. With medium blue sides together, sew the last square to row 1. Clip the seam allowances. Finger-press the seams open at each end. Make 18. Repeat to sew the last square to row 2 (medium blue sides together) and the last square to row 3.

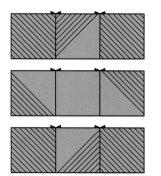

15. With medium blue sides together, sew rows 1, 2, and 3 together to complete the block. Clip the seam allowances. Finger-press the seams open at each end. Make 18 blocks.

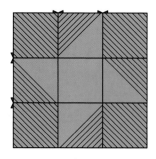

Make 18.

ASSEMBLING THE QUILT

Use a ½" seam allowance throughout the quilt construction. Refer to "Quilt Assembly" on page 27 for tips on sewing through the multiple layers created when seaming pieces together. Use the chenille cuts as a guide when clipping the seam allowances.

1. Arrange three Nine Patch Star blocks and two solid chenille blocks medium blue sides up as shown. With the medium blue sides together, sew the blocks together. Clip the seam allowances and finger-press the seams open at each end. Make four rows and label them rows *1, 3, 5,* and *7.*

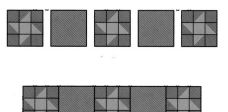

Make 4
(rows 1, 3, 5, and 7).

2. Arrange three solid chenille blocks and two Nine Patch Star blocks medium blue sides up as shown. With the medium blue sides together, sew the blocks together. Clip the seam allowances and finger-press the seams open at each end. Make three rows and label them rows *2, 4,* and *6.*

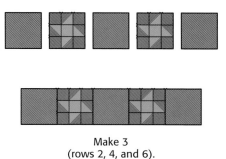

Make 3
(rows 2, 4, and 6).

3. Referring to the quilt diagram below, arrange the rows from steps 1 and 2, alternating them as shown. With the medium blue sides together, sew the rows together. Clip the seam allowances and finger-press the seams open at each end.

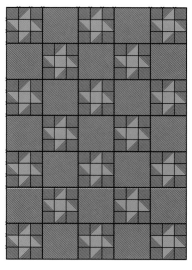

Quilt diagram

FINISHING THE QUILT

Refer to "Finishing" on page 28 for instructions on making and applying the dark blue straight-of-grain binding, and washing and drying the quilt.

STAR OF THE SHOW

Made by Amy Whalen Helmkamp

❖❖❖❖❖❖❖❖❖❖❖❖❖❖❖❖❖❖❖❖❖❖❖

You'll be the "star of the show" when you present this beauty to its recipient. This simple yet dramatic look is easily achieved—and so impressive. The floral and vine appliqué borders are also simple to make, using chenille strips for the vines, and fusible web and raw-edge appliqué for the flowers and leaves. Using yo-yos for the flower centers adds just the right finishing touch.

❖❖❖❖❖❖❖❖❖❖❖❖❖❖❖❖❖❖❖❖❖❖❖

Finished Quilt: 55" x 69" (before washing)
Finished Block: 15" x 15"

FRONT SIDE

REVERSE SIDE

MATERIALS

All yardages are based on 42"-wide fabric. **Do not prewash fabrics unless otherwise noted.**

- 4 yards of muslin for border filler*
- 2½ yards of muslin for block filler (optional)
- 2⅞ yards of beige print for filler and flower appliqués
- 2⅞ yards of medium pink print for filler and flower appliqués
- 2½ yards of light pink large-scale floral print for blocks
- 2½ yards of light moss green large-scale floral print for blocks
- 1¾ yards of dark moss green small-scale floral print for borders
- 1¾ yards of red tone-on-tone print for borders
- 1 yard of dark green small-scale print for chenille strips, leaf appliqués, and binding
- ⅜ yard of medium green small-scale print for chenille strips and leaf appliqués
- 1 fat quarter (18" x 21") of medium yellow mottled print for yo-yo flower centers
- 3 spools of thread, each 500 meters (547 yards), in a coordinating color
- 1¼ yards of fusible web
- Thread to match appliqués
- Refer to "Other Supplies" on page 14.

Prewash this fabric before cutting.

CUTTING

Cut all strips across the width of the fabric (selvage to selvage) unless instructed otherwise.

From the light moss green large-scale floral print, cut:
5 strips, 16" x 42"; crosscut into 9 squares, 16" x 16"

From the beige print, cut:
5 strips, 16" x 42"; crosscut into 9 squares, 16" x 16" *

From the unwashed (optional) muslin fabric, cut:
5 strips, 16" x 42"; crosscut into 9 squares, 16" x 16"

From the medium pink print, cut:
5 strips, 16" x 42"; crosscut into 9 squares, 16" x 16" *

From the light pink large-scale floral print, cut:
5 strips, 16" x 42"; crosscut into 9 squares, 16" x 16"

From the medium green small-scale print, cut:
1 strip, 12" x 40"; crosscut into 2 strips, 12" x 20"

From the dark green small-scale print, cut:
1 strip, 12" x 42"; crosscut into 2 strips, 12" x 20"
7 strips, 2½" x 42"

From the *lengthwise grain* of the dark moss green small-scale floral print, cut:
2 strips, 12½" x 55"
2 strips, 5½" x 46"

From the *lengthwise grain* of the prewashed muslin, cut:
2 equal lengths of 2 yards each; from *each* length, cut:
    2 strips, 12½" x 55" (4 total)
    2 strips, 5½" x 46" (4 total)

From the *lengthwise grain* of the red tone-on-tone print, cut:
2 strips, 12½" x 55"
2 strips, 5½" x 46"

*Set the remaining fabric aside for the flower appliqués.

MAKING THE BLOCK

You'll make nine 15" squares for this quilt. The squares are then joined to make a single, large Ohio Star block. Each square is made up of five layers of fabric.

(The muslin layer is optional; eliminate it if you wish.) As you cut the chenille, *pay very close attention* to the number of layers you are cutting. You don't want to cut through the base layer.

Use a ½" seam allowance throughout the block construction. Use the chenille cuts as a guide when clipping the seam allowances. Refer to "Chenille Techniques and Formulas" on page 16 for guidance as needed.

Star Points

1. Layer a 16" green floral square right side down, a 16" beige square right side down, a 16" muslin square (optional), a 16" medium pink square right side up, and a 16" pink floral square right side up. Pin baste the layers. Make nine. Divide the blocks into two stacks: one with four blocks and one with five blocks. Label the first stack *square A* and the second stack *square B*. Set the B squares aside for now.

Make 9.

2. Use an erasable marker to draw a diagonal line from the upper-left corner to the lower-right corner on the pink floral side of each A square. Draw a second diagonal line from the lower-left corner to the upper-right corner. These will be your stitching guidelines.

Square A.
Make 4.

3. Referring to "Threads and Stitches" on page 12, use a walking foot to sew a line of secure stitching directly on each of the guidelines you marked in step 2.

4. Use an erasable marker to draw a line through the vertical center (8") and the horizontal center (8") of each stitched square from step 3 as shown. This second set of guidelines will indicate the pivot points for the subsequent rows of chenille stitching.

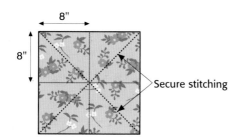

5. Continue sewing rows of *regular* straight stitching (not secure stitching) parallel to the guidelines you secure-stitched in step 3. Space the rows ⅜" apart. When the stitching reaches the lines you marked in step 4, pivot and then continue sewing, following the mirror-image line of secure stitching. Repeat in each large triangle of each A block.

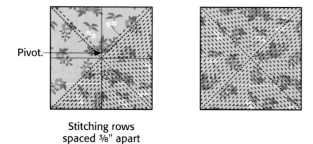

Stitching rows
spaced ⅜" apart

6. On the pink floral side of each A square, cut the center of the ⅜"-wide channels in two opposing triangles through *the top four layers only (three layers if you omitted the muslin layer).*

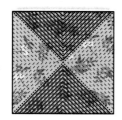

Square A, pink side.
Cut the center of the ⅜"-wide
channels. Make 4.

7. On the green floral side of each A square, cut the center of the ⅜"-wide channels in the two remaining triangles through *the top four layers only (three layers if you omitted the muslin layer).*

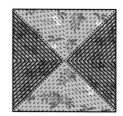

Square A, green side.
Cut the center of the ⅜"-wide
channels. Make 4.

Solid Chenille Squares

1. Use an erasable marker to draw a diagonal line from the upper-left corner to the lower-right corner on the pink floral side of each B block. This will be the stitching guideline.

Square B.
Make 5.

2. Select one marked B square. Use a walking foot to sew a line of stitching directly on the guideline you marked in step 1. Continue sewing rows of stitching parallel to the guideline. Space the rows of stitching ⅜" apart. Repeat for all B squares.

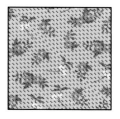

Stitch rows ⅜" apart.

3. Select one stitched block from step 2. On the pink floral side, cut through *the top four layers only (three layers if you omitted the muslin)*. Cut the center of the ⅜"-wide channels.

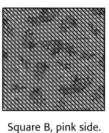

Square B, pink side.
Cut the center of the
⅜"-wide channels.
Make 1.

4. Using the remaining four stitched blocks from step 2, cut through *the top four layers only (three layers if you omitted the muslin)* on the green floral side. Cut the center of the ⅜"-wide channels.

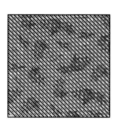

Square B, green side.
Cut the center of the
⅜"-wide channels.
Make 4.

MAKING THE CHENILLE STRIPS

Refer to "Making Chenille Strips" on page 24 for guidance as needed.

1. Layer a 12" x 20" dark green strip right side up and a 12" x 20" medium green strip right side up. Repeat to make a total of four layers. Pin baste the layers.

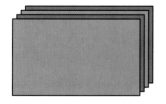

2. Use an erasable marker to mark the bottom edge of the top (medium green) strip 12" from the lower-left corner. Draw a diagonal line from the upper-left corner to this mark as shown. This will be your stitching guideline.

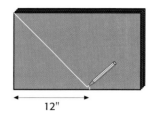

12"

3. Use a walking foot to sew a line of stitching directly on the guideline you marked in step 2. Stitch 13 additional rows to the right of the guideline. Space the rows ⅜" apart.

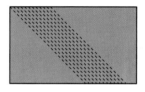

Stitch rows ⅜" apart.

4. Cut 3/16" to the left of the guideline row of stitching, cutting through *all layers of the fabric*. Set the lower-left triangle of the fabric sandwich aside for the leaf appliqués.

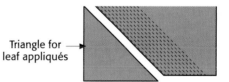

Triangle for
leaf appliqués →

5. Using the stitched piece of the unit from step 4, cut the center of the ⅜"-wide channels until you've cut a total of 14 strips. Trim the ends of each strip. You'll use these strips for the appliquéd vines.

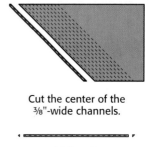

Cut the center of the
⅜"-wide channels.

Make 14.

MAKING THE FLOWER AND LEAF APPLIQUÉS

Refer to "Creating Appliqués" on page 23 and "Making Yo-Yos" on page 24 for guidance as needed.

1. Use the patterns on page 63 to trace 10 small leaves, 16 large leaves, and 10 flowers onto the fusible web. Cut out the shapes and follow the manufacturer's instructions to prepare and cut: 5 small leaves using the medium green print, 5 small leaves using the dark green print, 8 large leaves using the medium green print, 8 large leaves using the dark green print, 4 flowers using the beige print, and 6 flowers using the medium pink print.

2. Use the medium yellow print to make ten 2" yo-yos.

◇ ◇

Flower Variation

If you prefer, omit the yo-yo flower centers and use the placement circle for the yo-yo on page 63 to make appliquéd flower centers.

◇ ◇

MAKING THE BORDERS

You'll make four borders for this quilt. Each border consists of four layers of fabric. You'll appliqué the chenille-strip vines and the leaf and flower appliqués to the borders.

Top and Bottom Borders

1. Layer a 12½" x 55" dark moss green strip right side down, two 12½" x 55" prewashed muslin strips, and a 12½" x 55" red strip right side up. Pin baste generously to secure the layers during the appliqué process. Make two.

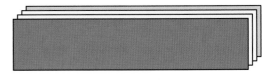

Make 2.

2. Referring to the photo on page 55 and the diagram below, draw an undulating line through the center of the red strip in each pin-basted border from step 1. This is the placement line for the chenille-strip vine.

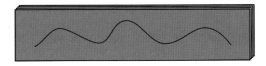

3. For each border, place five flower appliqués along the line drawn in step 2, alternating the flower colors as shown. Fuse the flower appliqués in place. Using a straight stitch and thread to match the appliqués, stitch approximately 1/16" to 1/8" from the edge of each flower to secure. Stitch a yo-yo to the center of each flower.

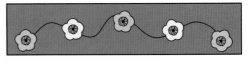

Top/bottom border

Stitching Option

To produce the look of embroidery on the reverse side of the border, use a triple straight stitch when sewing down the leaf, flower, and vine appliqués.

ASSEMBLING THE QUILT

Use a ½" seam allowance throughout the quilt construction. Refer to "Quilt Assembly" on page 27 for tips on sewing through the multiple layers created when seaming pieces together. Use the chenille cuts as a guide when clipping the seam allowances.

4. Appliqué the chenille strips, medium green side up, to cover the undulating lines you drew in step 2. Butt the ends of the strips next to the edges of the flower appliqués and sew the strips down, stitching from flower to flower and trimming the excess strip length as needed. Repeat until the vine is complete on both borders.

5. Referring to the photo on page 55, fuse and stitch eight large leaf appliqués to each border as shown.

Side Borders

1. Repeat "Top and Bottom Borders," step 1, on page 60 to layer the 5½" x 46" dark moss green, prewashed muslin, and red strips; pin baste.

2. Referring to the photo on page 55 and the diagram below, draw an undulating line through the center of the red strip in each pin-basted border from step 1. This will be the placement line for the chenille-strip vine.

3. Appliqué the chenille strips, medium green side up, to cover the undulating lines you drew on each border in step 2. Referring to the photo, fuse and stitch five small leaf appliqués to each border.

1. Arrange the nine squares floral pink side up in three rows of three squares each as shown. Pay close attention to the direction of the cuts on each cut square and the direction of the rows of stitching on the uncut squares as well.

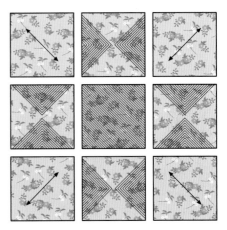

Arrows indicate the direction of stitching.

2. Beginning with row 1, place the first two squares with pink floral sides together and sew them together. Clip the seam allowances. Finger-press the seams open at each end. Repeat to sew the first two squares of row 2 and the first two squares of row 3 together as shown.

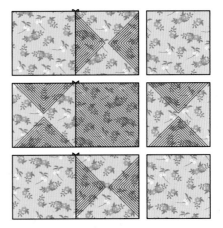

3. With pink floral sides together, sew the last square to row 1. Clip the seam allowances. Finger-press the seams open at each end. Repeat to sew row 2 and row 3.

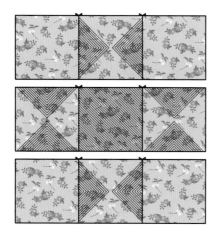

4. With pink floral sides together, sew rows 1, 2, and 3 together to complete the block. Clip the seam allowances. Finger-press the seams open at each end.

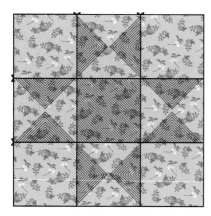

"This simple yet dramatic look is easily achieved."

5. With the appliquéd sides of the border and the green floral side of the quilt top together, sew the side borders to the sides of the quilt. Clip the seam allowances and finger-press the seams open at each end.

6. Repeat step 5 to sew the top and bottom borders to the top and bottom of the quilt. Clip the seam allowances and finger-press the seams open at each end.

Quilt diagram

FINISHING THE QUILT

Refer to "Finishing" on page 28 for instructions on making and applying the dark green straight-of-grain binding, and washing and drying the quilt.

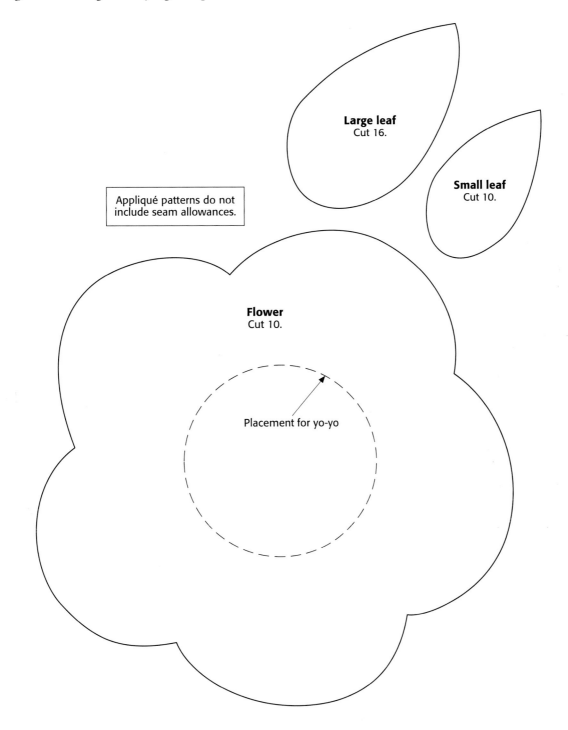

Large leaf
Cut 16.

Small leaf
Cut 10.

Appliqué patterns do not include seam allowances.

Flower
Cut 10.

Placement for yo-yo

DECK OF CARDS

Made by Valorie Scheer and Audrey Vorich

✧✧✧✧✧✧✧✧✧✧✧✧✧✧✧✧✧✧✧✧✧✧✧✧

Do you know someone who is an enthusiastic card player? Deal them a game in which there are no losers. If you play your cards right, the recipient of this quilt will feel he or she has been dealt a winning hand every time the quilt is used for cuddling.

✧✧✧✧✧✧✧✧✧✧✧✧✧✧✧✧✧✧✧✧✧✧✧✧

Finished Quilt: 49" x 61" (before washing)
Finished Block: 12" x 12"

FRONT SIDE

REVERSE SIDE

MATERIALS

All yardages are based on 42"-wide fabric. **Do not prewash fabrics.**

- 6⅛ yards of black mottled print for blocks
- 6⅛ yards of red mottled print for blocks
- ½ yard *total* of assorted red prints for appliqués
- ½ yard *total* of assorted black prints for appliqués
- 2 spools *each* of red and black thread, each 500 meters (547 yards)
- 1 yard of fusible web
- Refer to "Other Supplies" on page 14.

CUTTING

Cut all strips across the width of the fabric (selvage to selvage).

From the red mottled print, cut:
5 strips, 14" x 42"; crosscut into 10 squares, 14" x 14"
10 strips, 13" x 42"; crosscut into 30 squares, 13" x 13"

From the black mottled print, cut:
5 strips, 14" x 42"; crosscut into 10 squares, 14" x 14"
10 strips, 13" x 42"; crosscut into 30 squares, 13" x 13"

MAKING THE BLOCKS

You'll make 20 blocks for this quilt. Each block is made up of four layers of fabric plus an appliqué. As you cut the chenille, *pay very close attention* to the number of layers you are cutting. You don't want to cut through the base layer.

Use the chenille cuts as a guide when clipping the seam allowances. Refer to "Chenille Techniques and Formulas" on page 16 for guidance as needed.

1. Layer a 14" red square right side down and three 13" red squares right side up, centering them so that ½" of the base layer extends all around. Pin baste the layers. Make 10.

Make 10.

2. Repeat step 1, substituting the 14" and 13" black squares for the red squares. Make 10.

Make 10.

3. Use an erasable marker to draw a diagonal line from the upper-left corner to the lower-right corner on the top (13" red) side of each unit from step 1. This will be your stitching guideline.

4. Select one marked red square. Use a walking foot to sew a line of stitching directly on the guideline you marked in step 3. Continue sewing rows of stitching parallel to the guideline. Space the rows of stitching ⅜" apart. Repeat for all marked red squares.

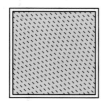

Stitch rows ⅜" apart.

5. On the top (13" red) side of each unit from step 4, cut the center of the ⅜"-wide channels through *the top three layers only.* Trim the excess base layer.

Cut the center of the ⅜"-wide channels.　　Make 10.

6. Repeat steps 3–5, substituting the 13" and 14" black squares for the red squares. Make 10.

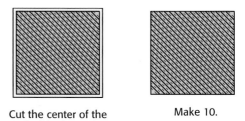

Cut the center of the ⅜"-wide channels.　　Make 10.

Appliqués

Refer to "Adding the Appliqués" on page 25 for guidance as needed.

1. Use the patterns on pages 69 and 70 to trace five spades, five clubs, five hearts, and five diamonds onto the fusible web. Cut out the shapes. Follow the manufacturer's instructions to prepare and cut five spades and five clubs using the assorted black scraps, and five hearts and five diamonds using the assorted red scraps.

2. Turn one red block, uncut side up, so the stitching runs from the upper-right corner to the lower-left corner as shown. Center and fuse one spade or club appliqué to the block. Repeat for all red squares.

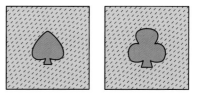

Make 5 each (10 total).

3. Repeat step 2, using the black squares and the red appliqués. Make 10 total.

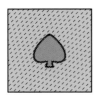

Make 5 each (10 total).

4. Using a close zigzag stitch (not a satin stitch) and thread to match the appliqués, stitch over the raw edges of the appliqués to secure them.

ASSEMBLING THE QUILT

Use a ½" seam allowance throughout the quilt construction. Refer to "Quilt Assembly" on page 27 for tips on sewing through the multiple layers created when seaming pieces together. Use the chenille cuts as a guide when clipping the seam allowances.

1. Place a Heart block, appliquéd side up, beside a Spade block, appliquéd side up. Place the Heart block on top of the Spade block and sew them together along the right edge. Clip the seam allowances. Finger-press the seam open at each end. Make three.

Make 3.

2. Place a Diamond block, appliquéd side up, beside a Club block, appliquéd side up. Place the Diamond block on top of the Club block and sew them together along the right edge. Clip the seam allowances. Finger-press the seam open at each end. Make three.

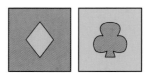

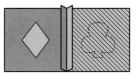

Make 3.

3. With black cut sides together, sew a unit from step 1 and a unit from step 2 together as shown to make a row. Clip the seam allowances. Finger-press the seams open at each end. Make three rows and label them rows *1, 3,* and *5.*

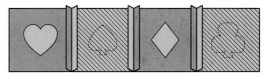

Make 3
(rows 1, 3, and 5).

4. Place a Spade block, red cut side up, beside a Heart block, black cut side up. Place the Spade block on top of the Heart block and sew them together along the right edge. Clip the seam allowances. Finger-press the seam open at each end. Make two.

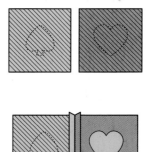

Make 2.

5. Place a Club block, red cut side up, beside a Diamond block, black cut side up. Place the Club block on top of the Diamond block and sew them together along the right edge. Clip the seam allowances. Finger-press the seam open at each end. Make two.

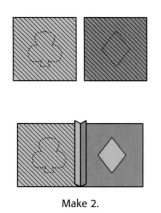

Make 2.

6. With black cut sides together, sew a unit from step 4 and a unit from step 5 together as shown to make a row. Clip the seam allowances. Finger-press the seams open at each end. Make two rows and label them rows *2* and *4*.

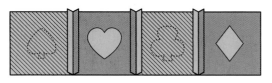

Make 2
(rows 2 and 4).

7. Referring to the quilt diagram below, arrange the rows from steps 3 and 6, alternating them as shown. With black cut sides together, sew the rows together. Clip the seam allowances. Finger-press the seams open at each end.

Quilt diagram

FINISHING THE QUILT

Refer to "Finishing" on page 28 for instructions on creating a rag-edge finish, and washing and drying the quilt.

"The recipient of this gift will feel he or she has been dealt a winning hand."

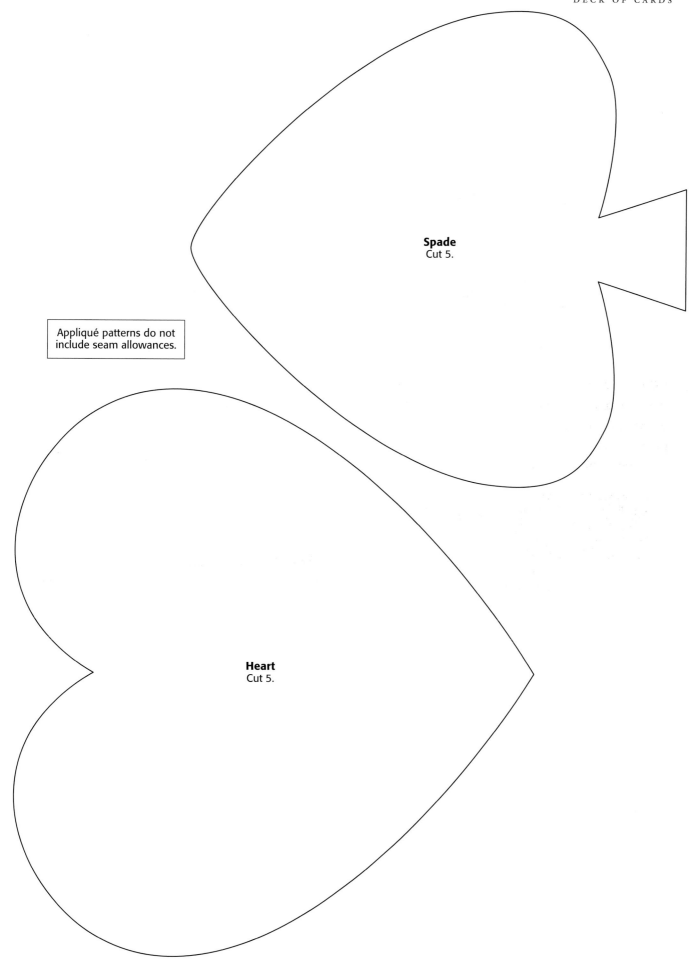

Spade
Cut 5.

Appliqué patterns do not
include seam allowances.

Heart
Cut 5.

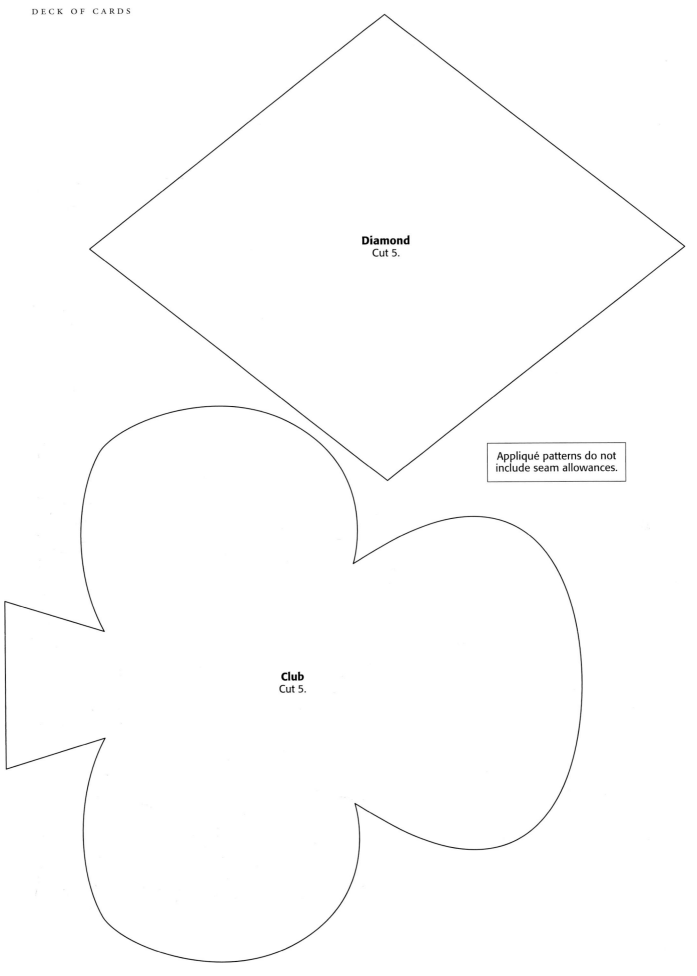

Diamond
Cut 5.

Appliqué patterns do not
include seam allowances.

Club
Cut 5.

BABY'S SNUGGLY

Made by Valorie Scheer

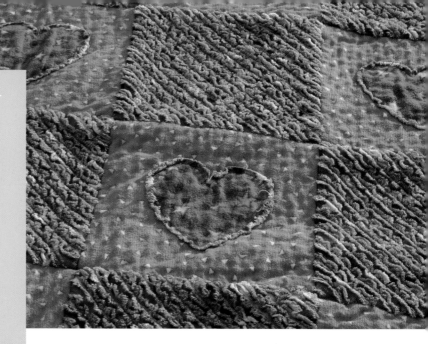

For that special little sweetheart or the newest little superstar, make a quilt that is soft, sweet, and cuddly. You'll want to make several of these quick and easy quilts to have on hand for those times when the happy announcement is made.

Finished Quilt: 36" x 43" (before washing)
Finished Block: 7" x 7"

FRONT SIDE

REVERSE SIDE

MATERIALS

All yardages are based on 42"-wide fabric. **Do not prewash fabrics.**

- 2⅓ yards of green print flannel for blocks and appliqués
- 2⅓ yards of yellow print flannel for blocks and appliqués
- 2 yards of off-white flannel for blocks
- 1 yard of blue print flannel for blocks
- 1 yard of pink print flannel for blocks
- ⅞ yard of coordinating narrow-striped flannel for binding
- 1 spool of thread, 500 meters (547 yards), in a coordinating color
- Thread to match appliqués
- Refer to "Other Supplies" on page 14.

CUTTING

Cut all strips across the width of the fabric (selvage to selvage) unless instructed otherwise.

From the off-white flannel, cut:
8 strips, 9" x 42"; crosscut into 30 squares, 9" x 9"

From *each* of the green and yellow print flannels, cut:
6 strips, 8" x 42"; crosscut into 30 squares, 8" x 8" (60 squares total)*

From the blue print flannel, cut:
3 strips, 8" x 42"; crosscut into 15 squares, 8" x 8"

From the pink print flannel, cut:
3 strips, 8" x 42"; crosscut into 15 squares, 8" x 8"

From the coordinating narrow-striped flannel, cut:
2½"-wide bias strips to equal 168"**

Set the remaining fabric aside for the heart appliqués.
**You must cut these strips on the bias for the stripes to run diagonally. Refer to "Bias Binding" on page 30 for guidance as needed.*

MAKING THE BLOCKS

You'll make 30 blocks for this quilt. Each block is made up of four layers of flannel plus an appliqué. As you cut the chenille, *pay very close attention* to the number of layers you are cutting. You don't want to cut through the base layer.

Use the chenille cuts as a guide when clipping the seam allowances. Refer to "Chenille Techniques and Formulas" on page 16 for guidance as needed.

1. Layer a 9" off-white square and two 8" green squares right side up, centering them so that ½" of the base layer extends all around. Pin baste the layers. Make 15 and label them *block A*.

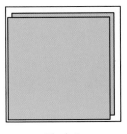

Block A.
Make 15.

2. Repeat step 1, substituting the 8" yellow squares for the green squares. Make 15 and label them *block B.*

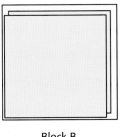

Block B.
Make 15.

3. Use an erasable marker to draw a diagonal line from the upper-left corner to the lower-right corner on the yellow/green side of each A and B block. This will be your stitching guideline.

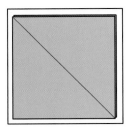

4. Select one marked A block. Use a walking foot to sew a line of stitching directly on the guideline you marked in step 3. Continue sewing rows of stitching parallel to the guideline as shown. Space the rows of stitching ½" apart. Repeat for all A and B blocks.

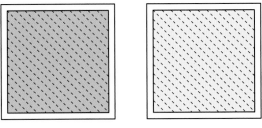

Stitching rows spaced ½" apart

5. On the green side of each A block, cut the center of the ½"-wide channels through *the top two layers only.* Trim the excess base layer. Make 15.

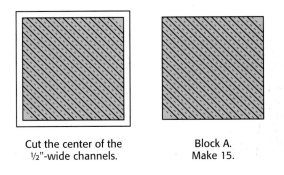

Cut the center of the
½"-wide channels.

Block A.
Make 15.

6. On the yellow side of each B block, cut the center of the ½"-wide channels through *the top two layers only.* Trim the excess base layer. Make 15.

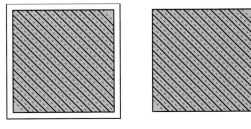

Cut the center of the
½"-wide channels.

Block B.
Make 15.

"Make a quilt that is soft, sweet, and cuddly."

Appliqués

Refer to "Adding the Appliqués" on page 25 for guidance as needed. Use your preferred method for raw-edge appliqué.

1. Use the pattern on page 76 to trace and cut out 15 hearts using the green print and 15 hearts using the yellow print. (If you wish, you can mix in some—or all—star appliqués. The pattern is also on page 76.)

2. Turn one A block off-white side up so the stitching runs from the upper-right corner to the lower-left corner. Place an 8" blue square right side up on the off-white square. Pin together along the edges. Make 15.

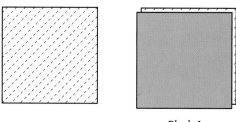

Block A.
Make 15.

3. Pin a yellow heart in the center of each A block, making sure to pin through all layers. Using a straight stitch and thread to match the appliqués, stitch ¼" from the raw edge of the heart to attach it to the quilt. Clip the raw edge, spacing the cuts ¼" apart. Make 15.

Block A.
Make 15.

Mix It Up

Want to mix things up a bit? Appliqué the green hearts to the blue squares and the yellow hearts to the pink squares.

4. Repeat steps 2 and 3, using the B blocks, the 8" pink squares, and the green hearts. Take care to orient the blocks correctly. Make 15.

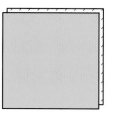

Block B.
Make 15.

ASSEMBLING THE QUILT

Use a ½" seam allowance throughout the quilt construction. Refer to "Quilt Assembly" on page 27 for tips on sewing through the multiple layers created when seaming pieces together. Use the chenille cuts as a guide when clipping the seam allowances.

1. Arrange three B blocks, appliqué side up, and two A blocks, green cut side up, as shown. With appliqué and green cut sides together, sew the blocks into rows. Clip the seam allowances. Finger-press the seams open at each end. Make three rows and label them rows *1, 3,* and *5.*

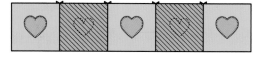

Make 3
(rows 1, 3, and 5).

2. Arrange three A blocks, green cut side up, and two B blocks, appliqué side up, as shown. With appliqué and green cut sides together, sew the blocks into rows. Clip the seam allowances. Finger-press the seams open at each end. Make three rows and label them rows 2, 4, and 6.

Make 3
(rows 2, 4, and 6).

3. Referring to the quilt diagram at right, arrange the rows from steps 1 and 2, alternating them as shown. With pink/appliqué and green cut sides together, sew the rows together into pairs. Clip the seam allowances and finger-press the seams open at each end. Make three pairs. Repeat to sew the pairs of rows together, clip the seam allowances, and finger-press.

Quilt diagram

FINISHING THE QUILT

Refer to "Finishing" on page 28 for instructions on making and applying the striped bias binding, and washing and drying the quilt.

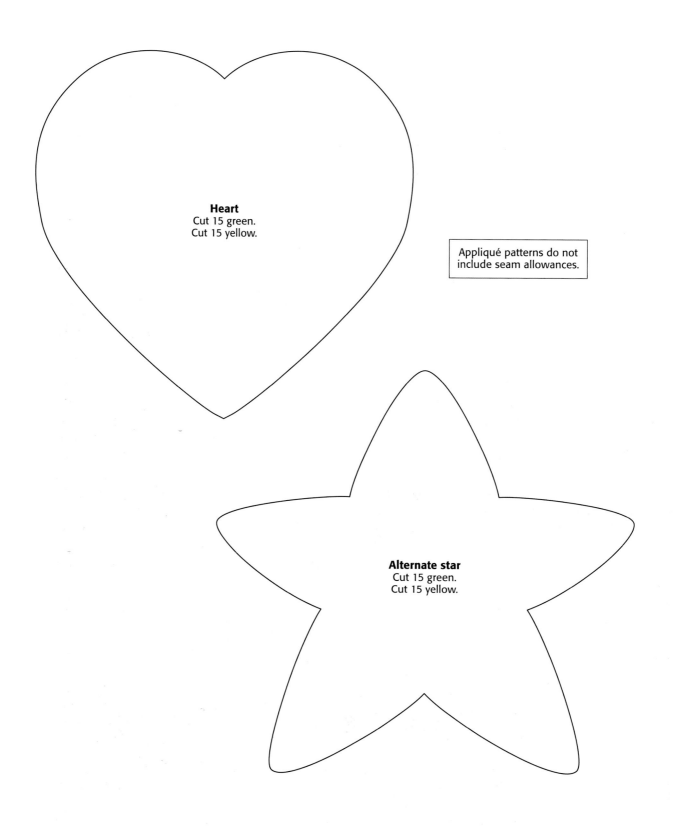

Heart
Cut 15 green.
Cut 15 yellow.

Appliqué patterns do not
include seam allowances.

Alternate star
Cut 15 green.
Cut 15 yellow.

SNOWBALL TILES

Made by Amanda Freeman

Snowballs aren't just for throwing; sometimes—as when they are sewn into a quilt—they are for giving warmth. Grab a cup of cocoa, cuddle up under these colorful snowballs, and let it snow, let it snow, let it snow!

Finished Quilt: 49" x 61" (before washing)
Finished Block: 12" x 12"

FRONT SIDE

REVERSE SIDE

MATERIALS

All yardages are based on 42"-wide fabric. **Do not prewash fabrics.**

- 2⅞ yards of off-white flannel for filler
- 1⅝ yards of flannel print with off-white background for blocks
- 1⅝ yards of red print flannel for blocks
- 1⅝ yards of flannel print with green background for blocks
- 1⅝ yards of blue print flannel for blocks
- ⅔ yard of medium green print flannel for block corners
- ⅔ yard of dark red print flannel for block corners
- ⅔ yard of beige print flannel for block corners
- ⅔ yard of medium blue print flannel for block corners

- ½ yard of coordinating flannel for binding
- 3 spools of thread, each 500 meters (547 yards), in a coordinating color
- Refer to "Other Supplies" on page 14.

CUTTING

Cut all strips across the width of the fabric (selvage to selvage).

From the flannel print with off-white background, cut:
4 strips, 13" x 42"; crosscut into 10 squares, 13" x 13"

From the off-white flannel, cut:
7 strips, 13" x 42"; crosscut into 20 squares, 13" x 13"

From the red print flannel, cut:
4 strips, 13" x 42"; crosscut into 10 squares, 13" x 13"

From the flannel print with green background, cut:
4 strips, 13" x 42"; crosscut into 10 squares, 13" x 13"

From the blue print flannel, cut:
4 strips, 13" x 42"; crosscut into 10 squares, 13" x 13"

From the medium green print flannel, cut:
4 strips, 4" x 42"; crosscut into 40 squares, 4" x 4"

From the dark red print flannel, cut:
4 strips, 4" x 42"; crosscut into 40 squares, 4" x 4"

From the beige print flannel, cut:
4 strips, 4" x 42"; crosscut into 40 squares, 4" x 4"

From the medium blue print flannel, cut:
4 strips, 4" x 42"; crosscut into 40 squares, 4" x 4"

From the coordinating flannel, cut:
5 strips, 2½" x 42"

MAKING THE BLOCKS

You'll make 20 blocks for this quilt. Each block is made up of three layers of flannel. If you are using any directional prints—such as the snowman fabrics in the quilt on page 77—pay special attention to the direction of the print to keep it upright. As you cut the chenille, *pay very close attention* to the number of layers you are cutting. You don't want to cut through the base layer.

Use a ½" seam allowance throughout the block construction. Use the chenille cuts as a guide when clipping the seam allowances. Refer to "Chenille Techniques and Formulas" on page 16 for guidance as needed.

1. Layer a 13" square with off-white background right side down, a 13" off-white square, and a 13" red square right side up. Pin baste the layers together. Make 10 and label them *block A.*

Block A.
Make 10.

2. Repeat step 1 using the 13" green squares, off-white squares, and blue squares. Make 10 and label them *block B.*

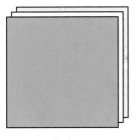

Block B.
Make 10.

3. Use an erasable marker to draw a diagonal line from the upper-right corner to the lower-left corner on the red side of each A block and on the blue side of each B block. This will be your stitching guideline. Measure 6¼" from the guideline in both directions and draw a diagonal line in the upper-left and lower-right corners of each block as shown. These lines will tell you where to stop stitching.

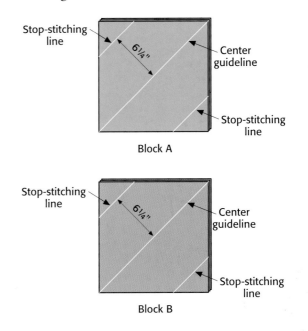

Block A

Block B

4. Select one A block. Use a walking foot to sew a line of stitching directly on the center guideline you marked in step 3. Continue sewing rows of stitching parallel to the guideline. Space the rows of stitching ⅜" apart. Stop sewing when you reach the diagonal lines in the corners. Repeat for all A and B blocks.

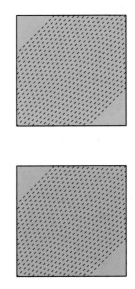

Stitch rows ⅜" apart.

5. On the red side of each A block, cut the center of the ⅜"-wide channels through *the top two layers only.* Make 10.

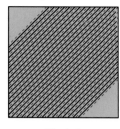

Block A.
Cut the center of the
⅜"-wide channels.
Make 10.

6. On the blue side of each B block, cut the center of the ⅜"-wide channels through *the top two layers only.* Make 10.

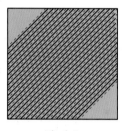

Block B.
Cut the center of the
⅜"-wide channels.
Make 10.

Attaching the Corners

1. Place a block A with the off-white side up. Place a 4" medium green square right side down in the upper-left and lower-right corners; pin. Place a 4" dark red square right side down in the lower-left and upper-right corners; pin. Make 10.

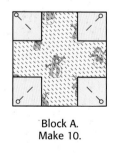

Block A.
Make 10.

2. Turn the block over so the red side is face up. Place a 4" beige square right side down in the upper-left and lower-right corners; pin. Place a 4" medium blue square right side down in the lower-left and upper-right corners; pin. Make 10.

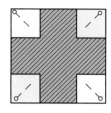

Reverse side of block A

3. Place a B block with the green side up. Place a 4" beige square right side down in the upper-left and lower-right corners; pin. Place a 4" medium blue square right side down in the lower-left and upper-right corners; pin. Make 10.

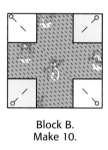

Block B.
Make 10.

4. Turn the block over so the blue side is face up. Place a 4" medium green square right side down in the upper-left and lower-right corners; pin. Place a 4" dark red square right side down in the lower-left and upper-right corners; pin. Make 10.

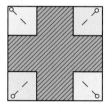

Reverse side of block B

5. Draw a diagonal line from corner to corner on each small corner square on one side of each A and B block as shown.

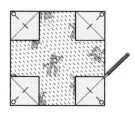

6. Select one A block. Use a walking foot to sew directly on the lines marked in step 5. Repeat for each A and B block.

7. Press the outside half of each corner square toward the block center on both sides of each A and B block. Trim off the corners of the block as shown, leaving a ¼" seam allowance. Press the small squares back toward the corner of the blocks. Make 20.

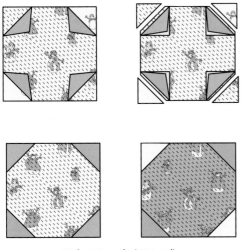

Make 10 each (20 total).

ASSEMBLING THE QUILT

Use a ½" seam allowance throughout the quilt construction. Refer to "Quilt Assembly" on page 27 for tips on sewing through the multiple layers created when seaming pieces together. Use the chenille cuts as a guide when clipping the seam allowances.

1. Place an A block, off-white side up, next to a B block, green side up, taking care to orient the corner triangles as shown. Place the B block on top of the A block and sew them together along the right edge. Clip the seam allowance. Finger-press the seam ends open. Make six.

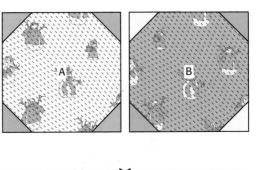

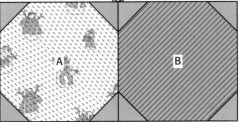

Make 6.

2. Place one unit from step 1, off-white/blue blocks face up, next to a unit with the green/red blocks face up. Place the green/red unit on top of the off-white/blue unit and sew them together along the right edge. Clip the seam allowances. Finger-press the seams open at each end. Make three rows and label them rows *1, 3,* and *5.*

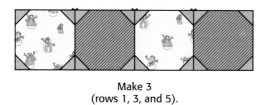

Make 3
(rows 1, 3, and 5).

3. Place a B block, blue side up, next to an A block, red side up. Place the A block on top of the B block and sew them together along the right edge, taking care to orient the corner triangles as shown. Clip the seam allowance. Finger-press the seam ends open. Make six.

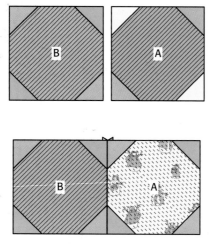

Make 6.

4. Place one unit from step 3 with the blue/off-white blocks face up next to a unit with the red/green blocks face up. Place the red/green unit on top of the blue/off-white unit and sew them together along the right edge. Clip the seam allowances. Finger-press the seams open at each end. Make two rows and label them rows *2* and *4.*

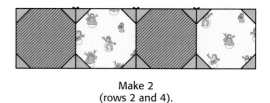

Make 2
(rows 2 and 4).

5. Referring to the quilt diagram below, arrange the rows from steps 2 and 4, alternating them as shown. With the off-white and blue sides together, sew the rows together. Clip the seam allowances and finger-press the seams open at each end.

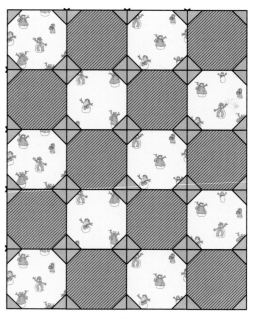

Quilt diagram

FINISHING THE QUILT

Refer to "Finishing" on page 28 for instructions on making and applying the coordinating straight-of-grain binding, and washing and drying the quilt.

GEESE ALL AROUND

Made by Isabel Lang

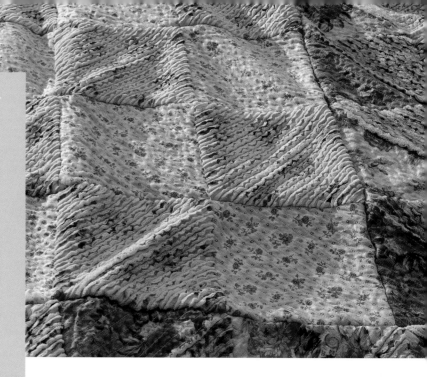

Patchwork geese circle round a patchwork field of pink and white in a design reminiscent of the fall migrations. Like those geese preparing for the onset of winter, you'll grab this cozy cover to comfort you during the cold winter days and nights.

Finished Quilt: 49" x 61" (before washing)
Finished Block: 6" x 12" Flying Geese block
6" x 6" Center Square block

FRONT SIDE

REVERSE SIDE

MATERIALS

All yardages are based on 42"-wide fabric. **Do not prewash fabrics.**

- 6½ yards of osnaburg fabric for filler*
- 2⅜ yards of floral print with cream background for Flying Geese
- 2⅜ yards of floral print with moss green background for Flying Geese
- 1⅜ yards of small-scale floral print with cream background for center squares
- 1⅜ yards of small-scale floral print with pink background for center squares

*If you wish, you may substitute unbleached muslin.

- 3 spools of thread, each 500 meters (547 yards), in a coordinating color
- Refer to "Other Supplies" on page 14.

CUTTING

Cut all strips across the width of the fabric (selvage to selvage).

From the floral print with cream background, cut:
6 strips, 13" x 42"; crosscut into 28 rectangles, 7" x 13"

From the osnaburg, cut:
12 strips, 13" x 42"; crosscut into 56 rectangles, 7" x 13"
10 strips, 7" x 42"; crosscut into 48 squares, 7" x 7"

From the floral print with moss green background, cut:
6 strips, 13" x 42"; crosscut into 28 rectangles, 7" x 13"

From the small-scale floral print with cream background, cut:
3 strips, 8" x 42", crosscut into 12 squares, 8" x 8"
3 strips, 7" x 42", crosscut into 12 squares, 7" x 7"

From the small-scale floral print with pink background, cut:
3 strips, 8" x 42"; crosscut into 12 squares, 8" x 8"
3 strips, 7" x 42"; crosscut into 12 squares, 7" x 7"

MAKING THE BLOCKS

You'll make 28 Flying Geese blocks and 24 center-square blocks for this quilt. Each Flying Geese and center-square block is made up of four layers of fabric. As you cut the chenille, *pay very close attention* to the number of layers you are cutting. You don't want to cut through the base layer.

Use a ½" seam allowance throughout the block construction. Use the chenille cuts as a guide when clipping the seam allowances. Refer to "Chenille Techniques and Formulas" on page 16 for guidance as needed.

Flying Geese Blocks

1. Layer a 7" x 13" cream rectangle right side down, two 7" x 13" osnaburg rectangles, and a 7" x 13" cream rectangle right side up. Pin baste the layers. Make 14 and label them *block A*.

Block A.
Make 14.

2. Repeat step 1, substituting 7" x 13" green rectangles for the cream rectangles. Make 14 and label them *block B*.

Block B.
Make 14.

3. Use an erasable marker to draw a line through the vertical center (6½") of each A and B block. Measure and mark a point on this line ½" from the top edge of the block.

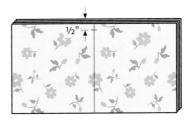

Block A

Block B

4. On each A and B block, draw a diagonal line from each bottom corner to the point marked in step 3. These will be your stitching guidelines.

Block A

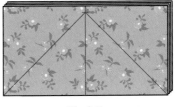

Block B

5. Select one A block. Referring to "Threads and Stitches" on page 12, use a walking foot to sew a line of secure stitching directly on the guidelines you marked in step 4. When the stitching reaches the ½" mark, pivot and continue sewing, following the mirror-image line of guideline stitching. Continue sewing rows of *regular* stitching (not secure stitching) parallel to the guidelines. Space

the rows of stitching ⅜" apart. When sewing the rows inside the triangle, sew to the centerline, pivot, and continue sewing parallel to the opposite guideline. Repeat for all A and B blocks.

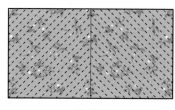

Block A.
Stitch rows ⅜" apart.

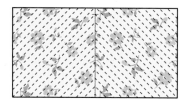

Block B.
Stitch rows ⅜" apart.

6. On one side of each A and B block, cut the center of the ⅜"-wide channels in the inner triangle through *the top three layers only.* Label this *side 1.*

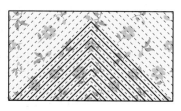

Block A, side 1.
Cut the center of the
⅜"-wide channels.
Make 14.

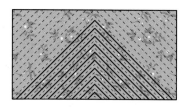

Block B, side 1.
Cut the center of the
⅜"-wide channels.
Make 14.

"You'll grab this cozy cover to comfort you during the cold winter days and nights."

7. On the reverse side of each A and B block, cut the center of the ⅜"-wide channels in the outer triangles through *the top three layers only.* Label this *side 2.*

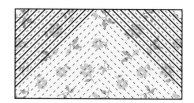

Block A, side 2.
Cut the center of the
⅜"-wide channels.
Make 14.

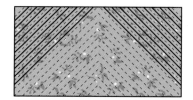

Block B, side 2.
Cut the center of the
⅜"-wide channels.
Make 14.

Center Square Blocks

1. Layer an 8" cream square right side down, two 7" osnaburg squares, and a 7" cream square right side up, centering them so ½" of the base layer extends all around. Pin baste the layers together. Make 12 and label them *block C.*

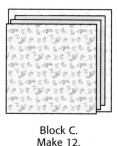

Block C.
Make 12.

2. Repeat step 1, substituting the 8" and 7" pink squares for the cream squares. Make 12 and label them *block D.*

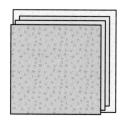

Block D.
Make 12.

3. Use an erasable marker to draw a diagonal line from corner to corner on one side of each C and D block. This will be your stitching guideline.

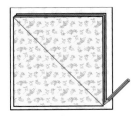

4. Select one C block. Use a walking foot to sew a line of stitching directly on this line. Continue sewing rows of stitching parallel to this guideline. Space the rows ⅜" apart. Repeat for all C and D blocks.

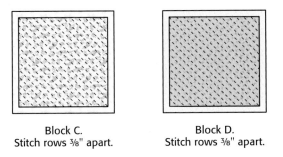

Block C.
Stitch rows ⅜" apart.

Block D.
Stitch rows ⅜" apart.

5. On the top (7") side of each C and D block, cut the center of the ⅜"-wide channels through *the top three layers only.* Trim the excess base layer.

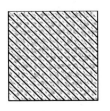
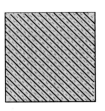

Block C.
Cut the center of the
⅜"-wide channels.

Block D.
Cut the center of the
⅜"-wide channels.

ASSEMBLING THE QUILT

Use a ½" seam allowance throughout the quilt construction. Refer to "Quilt Assembly" on page 27 for tips on sewing through the multiple layers created when seaming pieces together. Use the chenille cuts as a guide when clipping the seam allowances.

Quilt Center

1. Referring to the assembly diagram below, arrange the C blocks, cut side down, and the D blocks, cut side up, in six horizontal rows of four blocks each, alternating them as shown. With cut pink and uncut cream sides together, sew the blocks into rows. Clip the seam allowances. Finger-press the seams open at each end. Make three of each row.

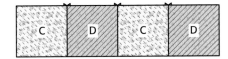
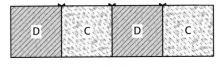

Make 3 each.

2. With cut pink and uncut cream sides together, sew the rows into pairs. Clip the seam allowances and finger-press the seams open at each end. Make three pairs. Repeat to sew the pairs of rows together, clip the seam allowances, and finger-press.

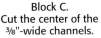

Make 3.

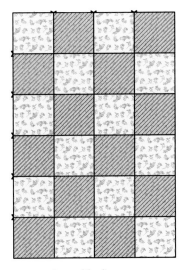

Assembly diagram

Flying Geese Borders

1. Place a B block, side 1 up, above an A block, side 1 up, as shown. Place the B block on top of the A block with sides 1 together and with the tip of the large triangle pointing in the opposite direction. Sew the blocks together. Clip the seam allowances. Finger-press the seam open at each end. Make 14.

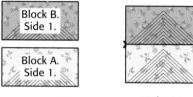

Block B.
Side 1.

Block A.
Side 1.

Make 14.

2. With sides 1 together, sew three units from step 1 together to make a side border as shown. Clip the seams. Finger-press the seams open at each end. Make two.

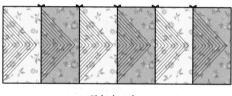

Side border.
Make 2.

3. With sides 1 together, sew four units from step 1 together to make a top border, carefully placing the end unit as shown. Clip the seams. Finger-press the seams open at each end. Repeat to make the bottom border. When the borders are attached, the flying geese will go clockwise around the quilt center.

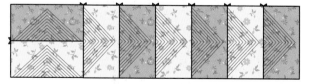

Top/bottom border.
Make 2.

4. With side 1 of each side border right sides together with the cut B blocks in the quilt center, sew the side borders to the quilt. Clip the seams. Finger-press the seams open at each end. Repeat to sew the top and bottom borders to the quilt.

Quilt diagram

FINISHING THE QUILT

Refer to "Finishing" on page 28 for instructions on how to create the rag-edge finish, and washing and drying the quilt.

FOR THE TABLE

Made by Randi Adym Helmkamp,
age 13

Decorate your table with something unique. Set the mood with fabrics that are formal or fun, and then finish with binding for an elegant look, or a rag edge for a casual look. Make one for each season or holiday.

Finished Table Runner:
13" x 49" (before washing)
Finished Placemat:
13" x 18" (before washing)
Finished Block: 12" x 12"

- 1 spool of thread, 500 meters (547 yards), in a coordinating color for blocks
- 1 spool of thread, 150 meters (164 yards), in a coordinating color for borders
- Refer to "Other Supplies" on page 14.

FRONT SIDE

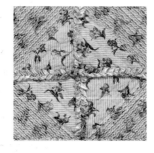

REVERSE SIDE

MATERIALS

*All yardages are based on 42"-wide fabric. **Do not prewash fabrics.***

- 3¼ yards of lavender metallic print for blocks, block filler, and place mat borders and filler
- 1⅛ yards of floral print with green stripe for blocks
- 1⅛ yards of floral print with cream background for blocks
- ⅝ yard of coordinating print for binding

Making Extra Place Mats

The yardage above will make the table runner and two place mats. For each additional pair of place mats, add:

- 1⅓ yards of lavender metallic print
- ½ yard of floral print with green stripe
- ½ yard of floral print with cream background
- ⅜ yard of coordinating print for binding

CUTTING

Cut all strips across the width of the fabric (selvage to selvage).

From the floral print with green stripe, cut:
5 strips, 7" x 42"; crosscut into 24 squares, 7" x 7"

From the lavender metallic print, cut:
10 strips, 7" x 42"; crosscut into 48 squares, 7" x 7"
2 strips, 13" x 42"; crosscut into 6 rectangles,
    7" x 13"
1 strip, 14" x 42"; crosscut into 2 rectangles, 8" x 14"

From the floral print with cream background, cut:
5 strips, 7" x 42"; crosscut into 24 squares, 7" x 7"

From the coordinating print, cut:
7 strips, 2½" x 42"

MAKING THE BLOCKS

You'll make four blocks for the table runner and one block for each place mat. Each block is made up of four squares. Each square consists of four layers of fabric. As you cut the chenille, *pay very close attention to the number of layers you are cutting.* You don't want to cut through the base layer.

Use a ½" seam allowance throughout the block construction. Use the chenille cuts as a guide when clipping the seam allowances. Refer to "Chenille Techniques and Formulas" on page 16 for guidance as needed.

1. Layer a 7" floral-stripe square right side down, a 7" lavender square right side down, a 7" lavender square right side up, and a 7" cream square right side up. Pin baste the layers together. Make 24.

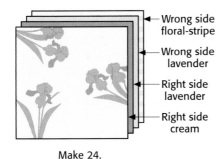

Make 24.

2. Use an erasable marker to draw a diagonal line from the upper-left corner to the lower-right corner on the cream side of each unit from step 1.

3. Select one marked unit from step 2. Referring to "Threads and Stitches" on page 12, use a walking foot to sew a line of secure stitching directly on the guideline. Continue sewing rows of *regular* straight stitching (not secure stitching) parallel to the guideline. Space the rows of stitching ⅜" apart. Repeat for all 24 squares.

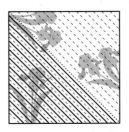

Stitch rows ⅜" apart.
Make 24.

4. On the cream side of each unit from step 3, cut the center of the ⅜"-wide channels on one half of the square *through the top three layers only.*

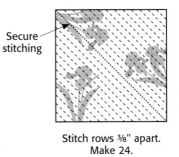

Cut the center of the
⅜"-wide channels.

5. Turn each square over and cut the center of the ⅜"-wide channels on the other half of the square *through the top three layers only.* When the quilt is washed, each side will look as though it were pieced with half-square triangles.

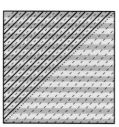

Cut the center of the ⅜"-wide channels.

6. Working with four squares at a time, arrange four squares, cream side up, so the cut sides create a center diamond as shown. Beginning with the top row, place the cream squares right sides together so the cut halves face each other. Sew the squares together. Clip the seam allowances. Finger-press the seams open at each end. Repeat for the bottom row.

7. Place the cream sides of two units from step 6 right sides together with the cut areas facing each other. Sew the units together. (Refer to "Quilt Assembly" on page 27 for a tip on sewing through multiple layers.) Clip the seam allowances using the chenille cuts as a guide. Finger-press the seams open at each end. Make six blocks.

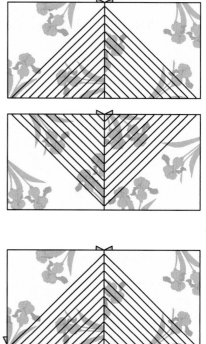

Make 6.

"Set the mood with fabrics that are formal or fun."

MAKING THE PLACE MAT BORDERS

You'll make two borders for each place mat. Each border consists of four layers of fabric. As you cut the chenille, *pay very close attention* to the number of layers you are cutting. You don't want to cut through the base layer.

1. Layer an 8" x 14" lavender rectangle right side down and three 7" x 13" lavender rectangles right side up, centering them so ½" of the base layer extends on all sides. Pin baste the layers together. Make two.

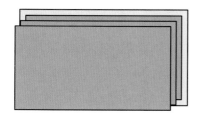

Make 2.

2. Measure the bottom edge of the top lavender rectangle and use an erasable marker to mark 7" from the lower-left corner. Draw a diagonal line from the upper-left corner to this mark. This will be your stitching guideline. Repeat for the other border unit.

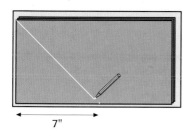

7"

3. Select one marked border unit. Use a walking foot to sew a line of stitching directly on the guideline. Continue sewing rows of stitching parallel to the guideline as shown. Space the rows ⅜" apart. Repeat for the other border unit.

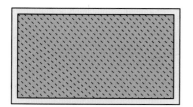

Stitch rows ⅜" apart.

4. On the top (13") lavender side of each border, cut the center of the ⅜"-wide channels through *the top three layers only.* Trim the excess base layer.

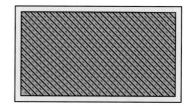

Cut the center of the
⅜"-wide channels.

5. On the 7" side, cut each border unit into two smaller rectangles, 3½" x 13". You'll have four border units total.

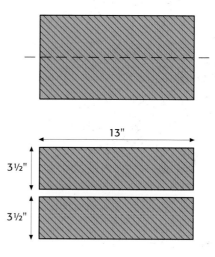

13"

3½"

3½"

ASSEMBLING THE TABLE RUNNER AND PLACE MATS

Use a ½" seam allowance throughout the project construction. Refer to "Quilt Assembly" on page 27 for tips on sewing through the multiple layers created when seaming pieces together. Use the chenille cuts as a guide when clipping the seam allowances.

Table Runner

With the cream sides together, sew the blocks in pairs. Make two pairs. Sew the pairs together to make a row. Clip the seams. Then finger-press the seams open at each end.

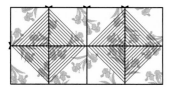

Make 2.

Place Mats

Place one border strip, cut side down, on the cream side of a remaining block, aligning the edges as shown. Sew the border strip to the block. Clip the seams. Finger-press the seams open at each end. Make two.

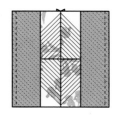

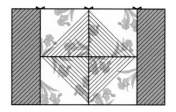

Make 2.

FINISHING THE TABLE RUNNER AND PLACE MATS

Refer to "Finishing" on page 28 for instructions on making and applying the coordinating print straight-of-grain binding, and washing and drying the table runner and place mats.

 Resources

You can find products recommended in this book at your local quilt shop or sewing store, or contact these companies for more information.

Clover Needlecraft Inc.
13438 Alondra Blvd.
Cerritos, CA 90703
www.clover-usa.com
Manufacturer of the Slash Cutter

G & K Craft Industries Ltd.
PO Box 38
Somerset, MA 02726
www.gkcraft.com
Manufacturer of Retayne and Synthrapol

J. T. Trading Corporation
458 Danbury Rd., Unit A18
New Milford, CT 06776
www.sprayandfix.com
Manufacturer of 505 Spray and Fix, a temporary fabric adhesive

Prym Consumer USA Inc.
PO Box 5028
Spartanburg, SC 29304
www.dritz.com
Distributor of Omnistrips and Dritz Electric Scissors

Roxanne International
742 Granite Ave.
Lathrop, CA 95330
www.thatperfectstitch.com
Manufacturer of Roxanne Glue-Baste-It

The Warm Company
954 E. Union St.
Seattle, WA 98122
www.warmcompany.com
Manufacturer of the Steam-A-Seam line of products

Meet the Author

I first discovered my love of sewing as a young girl, when my mother helped form a 4-H group for my friends and me. As I grew, my mother taught me crafts such as crochet, knitting, and painting, to name just a few. In the 1970s she introduced me to quilting, and I found my passion. I began designing and selling patterns in 1998, had my first book published in 2000 by Martingale & Company, and was a guest on *Kaye's Quilting Friends.* For a few years I worked in a local quilt shop where I met quilters with many different tastes and styles. Listening to these quilters provided inspiration for my designs, sparking my desire to create projects that were innovative yet still contained a traditional element. I love to learn about new techniques and new tools that make quilting fun. Sharing this passion is my goal.

Amy Whalen Helmkamp